South Africa's New Era

Martin Meredith is a former correspondent in Africa for the London *Observer* and the London *Sunday Times* and a former research fellow at St Antony's College, Oxford, whose writing on Africa has been widely acclaimed. His main works include: an account of Rhodesia's UDI years, *The Past is Another Country* (André Deutsch, 1979; Pan 1980); a study of Black Africa in the post-war era, *The First Dance of Freedom* (Hamish Hamilton, London; Harper and Row, New York, 1984); and an account of South Africa in the post-war era, *In the Name of Apartheid* (Hamish Hamilton, London; Harper and Row, New York, 1988). He has served as a member of a special study group on South Africa at the Royal Institute of International Affairs, London, and as Africa editor of Oxford Analytica. He recently acted as co-ordinator for a special study on *Economic Integration in Southern Africa* for the African Development Bank, published in 1993. He is currently a director of the Specialist Advisory Group on Africa, a consultancy based in London, Johannesburg and Oxford.

The Specialist Advisory Group on Africa is a business, political and economic intelligence network. It provides strategic information and political analysis to help businesses make decisions in a climate of high opportunity and high risk.

Also by Martin Meredith

**The Past is Another Country
The First Dance of Freedom
In the Name of Apartheid**

MARTIN MEREDITH

South Africa's New Era

The 1994 Election

Mandarin

For Christina

A Mandarin Paperback
SOUTH AFRICA'S NEW ERA

First published in Great Britain 1994
by Mandarin Paperbacks
an imprint of Reed Consumer Books Ltd
Michelin House, 81 Fulham Road, London SW3 6RB
and Auckland, Melbourne, Singapore and Toronto

Copyright © Martin Meredith 1994
The author has asserted his moral rights

A CIP catalogue record for this title
is available from the British Library
ISBN 0 7493 1910 0

Printed and bound in Great Britain
by Cox & Wyman Ltd, Reading, Berks

This book is sold subject to the condition
that it shall not, by way of trade or otherwise,
be lent, resold, hired out, or otherwise circulated
without the publisher's prior consent in any form
of binding or cover other than that in which
it is published and without a similar condition
including this condition being imposed
on the subsequent purchaser.

Contents

Chronology   vi-vii
Map   viii-ix

1 Election Days   1
2 The Release of Mandela   4
3 The Road to Negotiations   21
4 From Breakdown to Breakthrough   43
5 Interregnum   70
6 The Interim Constitution   97
7 Parties and Policies   109
   African National Congress   109
   National Party   134
   Pan-Africanist Congress of Azania   154
   Inkatha Freedom Party   158
   Democratic Party   159
   Freedom Front   160
   Fringe parties   162
8 The Campaign Trail   164
9 The Election Result   184
10 Profiles   189
11 The New Agenda   201

Appendix: Members of the Government of National Unity (May 1994)   216
Acknowledgements   224

Chronology

1910	Union of South Africa formed from the former Boer republics of Transvaal and the Orange Free State and the British colonies of the Cape and Natal
1912	South African Native National Congress formed, later to be called African National Congress
1914	National Party formed
1918	Nelson Mandela born
1921	Communist Party of South Africa formed
1936	F. W. de Klerk born
1948	National Party wins election
1950	Communist Party of South Africa banned
1952	Defiance Campaign launched, with Mandela as leader
1955	Congress of the People adopts the Freedom Charter
1957	Treason Trial begins, lasts four years
1959	Pan-Africanist Congress formed
1960	Sharpeville massacre ANC and PAC banned
1961	South Africa declared a republic Mandela heads ANC's new military wing, Umkhonto we Sizwe, launches sabotage campaign
1962	Mandela arrested, given five-year sentence
1963	Police raid Umkhonto headquarters at Rivonia farm outside Johannesburg

1964		Mandela sentenced to life imprisonment
1976		Soweto revolt
1982		Conservative Party formed
1983		United Democratic Front formed to fight new constitution
1984-86		Townships revolt, state of emergency
1985		Mandela turns down government's conditional offer of freedom
1988		Government effectively bans black opposition groups, including United Democratic Front
1989	July	President Botha meets Mandela
	Sept	De Klerk elected president
	Dec	De Klerk meets Mandela
1990	Feb	De Klerk lifts ban on ANC, PAC and Communist Party Mandela freed
	Aug	ANC suspends armed struggle
1991	Dec	Start of formal multiparty talks, Convention for a Democratic South Africa (Codesa)
1992	Mar	In a whites-only referendum, nearly 70 per cent vote for reform
	May	Codesa talks collapse
	June	ANC supporters killed at Boipatong
	Sept	Bisho massacre
1993	Apr	Multiparty talks resume
	July	Agreement on election date, Inkatha walks out
	Nov	Agreement on interim constitution
1994	Mar	South African government takes control of Bophuthatswana State of emergency in KwaZulu/Natal
	Apr	ANC wins South Africa's first democratic election
	May	Mandela's inauguration as president Government of National Unity formed

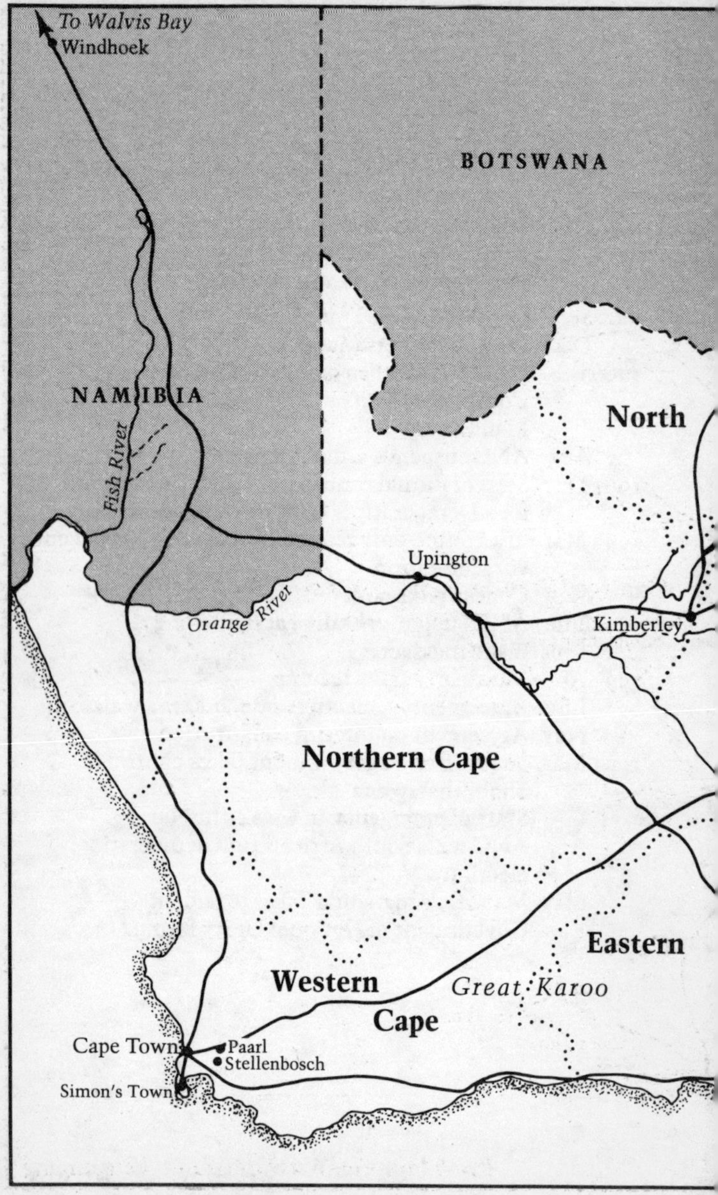
To Walvis Bay
Windhoek
BOTSWANA
NAMIBIA
North
Fish River
Upington
Orange River
Kimberley
Northern Cape
Eastern
Western
Great Karoo
Cape
Cape Town
Paarl
Stellenbosch
Simon's Town

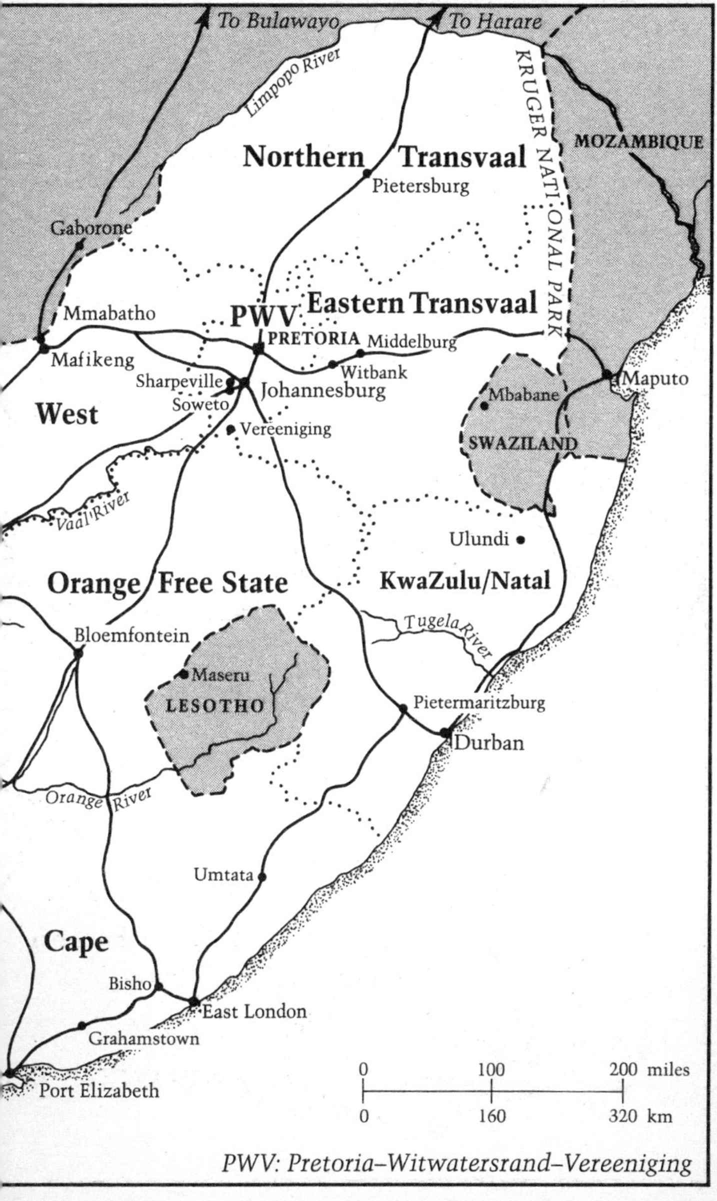

To Bulawayo
To Harare
Limpopo River
KRUGER NATIONAL PARK
MOZAMBIQUE
Northern Transvaal
Pietersburg
Gaborone
Eastern Transvaal
PWV
Mmabatho
PRETORIA
Middelburg
Mafikeng
Witbank
Sharpeville
Johannesburg
Soweto
Maputo
Mbabane
West
Vereeniging
SWAZILAND
Vaal River
Ulundi
Orange Free State
KwaZulu/Natal
Tugela River
Bloemfontein
Maseru
LESOTHO
Pietermaritzburg
Durban
Orange River
Umtata
Cape
Bisho
East London
Grahamstown
Port Elizabeth
0
100
200 miles
0
160
320 km
PWV: Pretoria–Witwatersrand–Vereeniging

I believe that the overwhelming majority of South Africans, black and white, hope to see the ANC and the government working closely together to lay the foundations for a new era in our country, in which racial discrimination and prejudice, coercion and confrontation, death and destruction will be forgotten.

Nelson Mandela, writing from prison to the South African government in 1989

Chapter 1

Election Days

In the early morning, as the sun rose over the green rolling hills of Natal, Nelson Mandela walked up the steps of the Ohlange High School hall in Inanda near Durban to cast his vote. His face wreathed in smiles, he greeted election officials before making his way to a polling booth to make his historic mark. Emerging from the polling station, he spoke of a future of hope, reconciliation and nation-building. 'It is,' he said, 'the beginning of a new era.'

Those days of voting in South Africa in April 1994 were memorable for all who participated in them. The birth of a democracy was an event which brought South Africans together in a manner which had never occurred before. The will to vote became a national will. Black and white citizens alike shared in a common determination to make it a success and in the sense of achievement when it was done. It was an event where the old, having cast their votes for the first time, said they could now die happy; and where the young knew that they stood at the threshold of a more propitious age; and about which all would be able to say: 'I was there.'

South Africa's 1994 election marked the end of the longest struggle for political rights in modern times. The importance of the occasion was all the greater since for so many years it had seemed that a peaceful end to the apartheid system was beyond reach and that a more likely outcome would be revolutionary war. Even in the weeks leading up to the election, the shadow of civil conflict had hung over the proceedings.

The sense of history in the making was evident to all who voted. In their millions they queued patiently for hours under the sun. Many had walked miles to reach a polling station; some arrived on crutches, some in wheelchairs; some were dressed in their Sunday-best clothes; some wore outfits they had made especially for the occasion. There were long delays as polling stations ran out of ballot papers. Many arriving in the early morning were still waiting to vote late in the afternoon, tired and frustrated; some in rural areas had to vote by candlelight. Yet still they remained patient, marking the event with a calmness rarely witnessed in South Africa's turbulent history. And when they finally returned home, having voted, it was with a sense of profound fulfilment, not just from participating in the election of a new government, but from exercising a right which had been denied to most South Africans for so long. Time and again, voters leaving polling stations spoke of how their dignity had been restored.

The election was marred by many incidents. Afrikaner extremists, *bittereinders*, resenting the loss of white political power, staged a series of bomb attacks, one in the centre of Johannesburg's business district, another at its international airport, killing 21 civilians and injuring nearly 200 others. But the effect was to increase the resolve of voters, not to deter them. The administration of the election, placed in the hands of inexperienced officials and workers, was woefully deficient, but it still managed to produce an acceptable result.

But the election was most notable for the outbreak of peace and goodwill it brought. The fever of violence which had afflicted the country for more than a decade abated. Even the killing fields of KwaZulu/Natal, where political warfare had caused more than 10,000 deaths since the mid-1980s, fell silent. On the Witwatersrand, members of rival factions found themselves side by side in the same queue in black townships, swopping complaints about the failings of the election administration. On each polling day, South Africa was more peaceful than it had been for many years.

For many whites, the experience of the election was as moving as it was for blacks. Madams joined their maids waiting patiently to vote, with a sense of their own liberation. Wealthy whites in the northern suburbs of Johannesburg, finding that queues were shorter in a nearby squatter camp, ventured there for the first time to cast their vote without the slightest qualm. The feelings of relief that the curse of apartheid had finally been lifted were as strong amongst the white community which had imposed it as it was on the blacks who had suffered under it.

All this, of course, was a honeymoon time. The tasks that lay ahead were daunting; the potential for conflict remained. But it was no less memorable for that. And it was a fitting tribute to the man who had spent 27 years in prison hoping for such an outcome and the Afrikaner leader who decided he should be released.

Chapter 2

The Release of Mandela

As a disciple of apartheid, Frederik Willem de Klerk possessed impeccable credentials. He came from a prominent Afrikaner family at the heart of the political establishment which had ruled South Africa since 1948. His father, Jan, had served as a cabinet minister under Hendrik Verwoerd, the architect of grand apartheid, whose schemes for the territorial separation of white and black were designed to rid South Africa of its black citizens and ensure permanent white supremacy. His uncle, J. G. Strydom, was a former prime minister well known for his aggressive insistence on white *baasskap* (mastery). Earlier generations too had made their mark as activists in the Afrikaner cause. The home environment in which the young de Klerk grew up, therefore, was steeped in the traditions of Afrikaner politics and history.

His career followed a predictable course. He played a leading role in student affairs at Potchefstroom University; set up a successful law practice in the Transvaal town of Vereeniging; observed the strict Calvinist traditions of the Gereformeerde Kerk; entered parliament in 1972, rose swiftly from the backbenches, and in 1978, at the age of 42, became the youngest member of John Vorster's cabinet.

What was most notable about his political style was his rigid loyalty to the National Party and all that it stood for. He conformed faithfully to every party policy of the time, whether it was under the mantle of Strydom, or Verwoerd, or Vorster, or subsequently, P. W. Botha. Over the years he had spoken out adamantly against integrated sport, mixed marriages, trade union rights for blacks and black claims for permanent residence in white South Africa. Above all, he was a forceful proponent of the National Party's policy on racial grouping, of keeping apart, by law wherever necessary, South Africa's four racial groups – white, blacks, Coloureds and Indians. In Botha's government, he was given control of the white 'own affairs' administration and projected himself as a zealous advocate of white interests, while acknowledging that blacks too had an equal right to run their own institutions. Whites, he said in 1989, must be guaranteed a 'community life, their own living areas, schools, institutions and systems ... This also means certainty over the definition of each group, and that each group should have its own power base and may decide together over community issues.' When the time came for the National Party parliamentary caucus to choose a new leader to succeed Botha in 1989, de Klerk was the favoured candidate of right-wing members.

From the vantage point of the president's office in Pretoria, however, de Klerk began a reassessment of South Africa's prospects. Since 1985, South Africa had been governed under successive states of emergency to enable the government to deal with internal revolt against apartheid. Black political organisations had been banned; thousands of dissidents had been detained; the army and paramilitary police had been used to crush township 'unrest'; and strict censorship had been imposed on the media. Abroad, South Africa was treated as a pariah state, shunned in international political circles and subjected to trade sanctions and sports boycotts. Foreign bankers had inflicted their own sanctions by refusing to provide new loans; and scores of foreign corporations had decided to withdraw from the country. From its headquarters in Lusaka, Zambia, the African National Congress was committed to bringing down the apartheid regime by revolutionary war and had infiltrated hundreds of guerrillas back across the border.

With the support of internal activists, its stated aim was to make black townships 'ungovernable'.

None of this presented insuperable difficulties for the government. Its security forces were more than a match for any threat either from township activists or trained guerrillas. Nor had it shaken the government's confidence in the merits of white rule. To P. W. Botha, it was all evidence of the 'total onslaught' he believed South Africa was facing and which he was determined to resist. His response had been to place ever more power in the hands of his officials on the State Security Council, giving them direct control over a vast range of government activity at every level of society across the entire country. In effect, South Africa was being ruled by security managers. Towards foreign critics, Botha had become increasingly contemptuous. South Africa, he declared, would not 'crawl before anyone' to avert the threat of sanctions and was quite prepared to 'go it alone'.

What struck de Klerk, in assessing the government's options, was the lack of any viable political strategy other than to rely on security management. Botha's decade in office had begun with high hopes of reform. Although by nature an authoritarian figure, ruthless, intolerant of opposition and no less committed to the cause of white supremacy than his predecessors, Botha had seen the need for more efficient management of the apartheid system. 'Adapt or die' was his message to the white population in his early years. Accordingly, the government lifted the ban on mixed marriages, recognised black trade union rights and finally accepted the permanent status of blacks in urban areas, allowing them property rights and withdrawing the hated 'pass law' system through which the police enforced control and checked the tide of migration from rural to urban areas. But Botha's reform strategy soon foundered. The centrepiece was a new constitution with a parliament divided into three chambers: a House of Assembly for whites; a House of Representatives for the mixed-race Coloured population; and a House of

Delegates for Indians. The whites were left firmly in control but could point to new allies in the Coloured and Indian communities. No representation was accorded to the black population. Botha's view was that blacks had been given sufficient political representation through the establishment of ten 'homelands' run by black governments, four of which had chosen 'independence' from South Africa. All that he was prepared to concede to urban blacks was elected local councils. The revolt which swept through South Africa's black townships in the mid-1980s rendered Botha's reform programme obsolete. His last years in office were marked by brutal repression at home and crude defiance of his critics abroad. He himself became increasingly irascible and isolated, a bitter old autocrat refusing to listen to advice and harbouring resentment against his own colleagues. In the end it was left to de Klerk to manoeuvre him out of office.

Botha's legacy was a country not only bereft of a viable political system but afflicted by deep economic malaise. Economic growth in the 1980s, at 1.5 per cent a year, had failed to keep pace with population growth, at 2.5 per cent a year. Living standards were in decline; unemployment was rising relentlessly. There was a dearth of new investment and a steady outflow of capital. The gold mining industry, upon which South Africa's prosperity had been founded, was in decline; its costs had become the highest in the world. The manufacturing sector, protected by high tariff walls, was uncompetitive in world markets. Throughout the economy there was a critical shortage of skills. Enormous resources had to be devoted to stockpiling oil and developing new energy sources to ward off the impact of sanctions. The costs of the apartheid system itself, in particular the vast bureaucratic structures needed to keep it in place, were a constant burden. Among other things, South Africa possessed 13 legislative assemblies, 18 departments of health and welfare, 14 departments of education, 14 departments of finance and 11 presidents, prime ministers or chief ministers.

Once in office, de Klerk was pragmatic enough to accept that apartheid had finally reached 'a dead end'. Unlike Botha, he saw no future in depending upon the security apparatus to defend white rule. The cycle of black opposition had become at each stage increasingly widespread and increasingly violent. Without political reform, it was bound to continue. The longer reform was delayed, the greater the danger ahead for the government. In the meantime, the prospects for economic recovery would steadily diminish. 'We had to escape from a corner where everything had stagnated into confrontation,' he remarked later. De Klerk calculated, on the basis of election results in September 1989, that two-thirds of the white electorate would support political reform provided that it was prudently managed. Within the National Party, a large body of MPs favoured change: nearly as many MPs had voted in 1989 for a candidate on the liberal wing to lead the party as had voted for de Klerk himself. The business community too constantly harped on about the need for reform. On his trips abroad as the new president, de Klerk was readily assured by foreign governments of support if he changed course. What also influenced him was the advice of senior figures in the Broederbond, the secretive Afrikaner organisation which in the 1930s had laid the foundations for the Afrikaners' quest for power but which in the 1980s had become an advocate for progressive reform and had opened secret contacts with ANC officials. 'The greatest risk is not to take any risks', was their assessment. Even de Klerk's own father, Jan, once so staunch a supporter of the apartheid regime, believed that the time had come to move on.

De Klerk's objective now became to secure a new dispensation which encompassed black demands for political rights but which gave the whites a powerful, even commanding, role in government – in effect to retain power but under different circumstances. He was confident that the plan he had in mind for 'power-sharing' amongst different racial groups would find sufficient allies to make it a viable proposition. All would depend on negotiation. The government, meanwhile, would remain firmly in control until it was satisfied with the deal which had been struck. All this still left de Klerk with awkward decisions to take over the release of Nelson Mandela and the role of banned organisations like the African National Congress.

Mandela had been sentenced to life imprisonment in 1964 for his part in organising armed rebellion against the apartheid regime. His trial, lasting nine months, had stirred interest around the world. What had gained particular attention was Mandela's dignified bearing and the impassioned defence he had made for launching Umkhonto we Sizwe, the armed wing of the ANC, formed after the movement had been banned in 1960. The decision had been taken, said Mandela, only after all channels of peaceful protest had been blocked by the government. In the aftermath of the trial, the government had done its best to erase the memory of him from the public mind by banning his speeches, prohibiting the reproduction of his photograph and shutting him away in a prison camp on Robben Island in Table Bay, five miles off the coast of Cape Town. Virtually no outsiders other than lawyers and members of his immediate family had been permitted to see him or talk to him, and when they were allowed, it was only under strict supervision. But the effect had been to increase Mandela's stature rather than to diminish it. Abroad, Mandela became one of the most famous prisoners in the world: songs were written about him, streets named after him, awards showered upon him. Reports of him which filtered out of Robben Island spoke of a man of immense authority and influence, still resilient after 20 years of prison life. In the early 1980s a campaign launched in South Africa for Mandela's release attracted support from white university students and liberal politicians as well as black organisations. Botha's response to the campaign was to denounce Mandela as an 'arch-Marxist', committed to violent revolution, who would have to serve the sentence imposed upon him by a court of law. By the mid-1980s, facing upheaval in black townships, Botha was prepared to offer Mandela's release from prison as a concession to black demands, but only provided he renounced violence. Mandela's defiant response was relayed to a mass rally at a stadium in Soweto in 1985 by his daughter, Zindzi: 'I cherish my own freedom dearly but I care even more for your freedom ... I am not less life-loving than you are. But I cannot sell the birthright of the people, to be free. I am in prison as the representative of the people and of your organisation, the African National Congress, which was banned. What freedom am I being offered whilst the organisation of the people remains banned? ... Only free men can negotiate.'

By 1989, Botha's last year in office, his dilemma about Mandela remained unresolved. Mandela, by then, was 70 years old; his imprisonment had lasted for more than 26 years. His living conditions in that time had improved markedly. In 1982 he had been moved from Robben Island to Pollsmoor maximum security prison on the mainland. But there was concern about his health. In 1988 he had been taken to a clinic for treatment for tuberculosis. He had since been moved to a comfortable bungalow in the grounds of Victor Verster prison-farm among the vineyards of Paarl, in the heartland of the Cape wine-growing district. The clamour for his release both at home and abroad had meanwhile become ever more insistent.

The government was well informed of Mandela's views about what steps needed to be taken. Since 1986, at Mandela's own instigation, he had held periodic meetings with government ministers and officials in an endeavour to persuade the government to negotiate with the ANC. Government ministers, seeking a way through the impasse in 1989, found his position as resolute as ever. But he was anxious to help break the fearful deadlock that gripped South Africa, as he made clear in a memorandum to Botha. 'The deepening political crisis in our country has been a matter of grave concern to me for quite some time,' he wrote in 1989. 'I now consider it necessary in the national interest for the African National Congress and the government to meet urgently to negotiate an effective political settlement.' The meeting would be the first major step towards lasting peace. 'Two political issues will have to be addressed at such a meeting: firstly, the demand for majority rule in a unitary state; secondly, the concern of white South Africa over this demand, as well as the insistence of whites on structural guarantees that majority rule will not mean domination of the white minority by blacks. The most crucial task which will face the government and the ANC will be to reconcile these two positions.' Mandela warned that his initiative was being taken at his own instigation because he had no means of consulting the ANC's leadership in Lusaka. But he hoped that the ANC would subsequently endorse his approach and meanwhile emphasised his position as 'a loyal and disciplined member of the ANC'. He addressed again the issue of violence. 'The position of the ANC on the question of violence is very simple. The organisation has no vested interest in violence. It abhors any action which may cause loss of life, destruction of property and misery to the people. It has worked long and patiently for a South Africa of common values and for an undivided and peaceful non-racial state. But we consider the armed struggle a legitimate form of self-defence against a morally repugnant system of government which will not allow even peaceful forms of protest.'

A new formula was now drawn up to provide for Mandela's release. Botha told parliament in April 1989 that he would no longer insist that Mandela should renounce violence as a political weapon. 'If he is prepared to contribute to a peaceful settlement of South Africa's future, I will personally welcome it, and the government would react open-heartedly,' he said. Three months later, Botha invited Mandela to take tea with him at his official residence at Cape Town. The meeting, termed officially as 'a courtesy call', was remarkably cordial. Mandela later described Botha as 'a charming man indeed', adding, 'The thing that impressed me was that he poured the tea'. No policy matters were discussed, no negotiations took place, no issue was made about Mandela's release. The symbolic importance of Botha sitting down with a prisoner whom he had hitherto denounced as a 'communist terrorist' was real enough. But Botha was still no nearer addressing the central issue of political reform that Mandela had raised in his memorandum. Nor could he stomach the notion of having to deal with the African National Congress.

Since its banning in 1960, the African National Congress had met with mixed fortunes. Its initial attempts to sustain political protest inside South Africa soon collapsed. The efforts of Mandela and his colleagues to organise armed rebellion through Umkhonto had also ended in failure. By the end of 1964 hardly any active revolutionaries remained at large in the country. In exile, the ANC succeeded in gaining diplomatic attention from foreign governments which had first become critical of South Africa as a result of the Sharpeville massacre in 1960, when 69 Africans were killed by police during an anti-apartheid protest. Support and recognition were forthcoming from Western governments and organisations as well as from the Eastern bloc, though it was the Soviet Union which had given most support, providing funds, equipment and training. The guerrilla camps which the ANC set up in Tanzania, one thousand miles away from the borders of South Africa, however, were more noted for internal disputes and dissension than for any revolutionary activity, making them easy prey for South African intelligence. When the Soweto revolt broke out in 1976, the ANC was nowhere to be found.

It nevertheless benefited from the resurgence of black protest inside South Africa from the mid-1970s. The ranks of Umkhonto in exile were swelled by a wave of thousands of eager recruits who left the country seeking to sign up for the revolution. Another advance came as a result of the collapse of Portuguese rule in Portugal's African colonies which opened the way for the ANC to establish guerrilla bases in Mozambique and Angola, closer to South African borders. ANC groups were set up in Botswana, Swaziland and Lesotho – 'forward areas', as they were called – to help establish an internal network and to supervise the flow of more recruits. In 1977 Umkhonto began a low-level sabotage campaign, not so much to threaten the economy or white security, but to re-establish a political following among the black population and to raise its morale. In the black townships, the underground existence of Umkhonto – or MK, as it was popularly known – helped inspire civil unrest and defiance.

The townships revolt lasting from 1984 to 1986 brought the ANC to ever greater prominence. From its headquarters in Lusaka, the ANC played only a marginal role in the upheaval, broadcasting inflammatory statements, urging blacks to make the townships ungovernable, but possessing few means itself of controlling, directing or even influencing the course of events. But at the forefront was the United Democratic Front (UDF), a conglomeration of community and youth organisations acting, in effect, as the ANC's internal representative. ANC flags, colours, slogans and songs testified to its everyday presence in township life. Opinion surveys indicated a vast potential following which cut across ethnic and tribal groups, regional differences, classes, age and education. Before falling victim to government repression, the UDF proved itself capable of rallying mass opinion on an unprecedented scale.

All this added to the ANC's credentials abroad. Its 40 'embassies' around the world already constituted a more widespread foreign 'representation' than that maintained by the South African government. Now even conservative Western governments, notably those led by President Reagan and Prime Minister Thatcher, were obliged to acknowledge that the ANC had become an indispensable factor in any attempt to achieve a negotiated settlement in South Africa. Celebrating its seventy-fifth anniversary in 1987, the ANC noted confidently how many countries and governments looked on the movement 'virtually as a government in waiting'.

Yet in terms of confronting the reality of white power in South Africa, the ANC had far less to show. Its guerrilla attacks were little more than an irritant, requiring only police counter-insurgency measures on the government's part. Even the ANC was prepared to concede they amounted to no more than 'armed propaganda'. Its foothold in the 'forward areas' was tenuous. Neighbouring states like Mozambique, faced with South African retaliation, were eventually forced to withdraw their support for guerrilla activity. By 1989, all Umkhonto camps had been removed far to the north again, to Tanzania. Left largely inactive, Umkhonto was rife with disputes and dissension; a mutiny among guerrillas in Angola was brutally repressed. As an internal document about the state of affairs in 1989 admitted: 'We do not have the capacity within our country to intensify the armed struggle in any meaningful way.'

Botha consequently was in no mood even to contemplate a meeting with the ANC. In his view, the ANC was an organisation under communist control bent on destroying white civilisation. It was at the centre of the 'total onslaught' the country was facing. Its links with the Soviet Union and other communist states; the support it received from Marxist regimes in Mozambique and Angola; above all, its alliance with the South African Communist Party (SACP); all were cited by Botha as evidence of the ANC's true nature. The only answer to this 'total onslaught' was 'total strategy'; and with this the government was already succeeding.

Botha, like his predecessors, was obsessed about the role of the SACP. It had been the first of the anti-apartheid organisations to be banned, in 1950, ten years before the

ANC was banned. It consisted of only a small cadre of white, African, Coloured and Indian members, but they were efficient, dedicated and wielded considerable influence among trade unions and organisations like the ANC. Communists had played a prominent role in helping to launch Umkhonto in 1961. The party's theory on revolution in South Africa, at that time, envisaged two stages. In the first stage, 'a united front of national liberation', consisting of a Communist Party alliance with the ANC through the military wing of Umkhonto, would set out 'to destroy white domination'. In the second stage, South Africa would be transformed into a socialist state. As one of the founders of Umkhonto, Mandela welcomed the help of communists. As he explained in his trial in 1964: 'For many decades communists were the only political group in South Africa who were prepared to treat Africans as human beings; who were prepared to eat with us, talk with us, live with us and work with us. They were the only political group which was prepared to work with the Africans for the attainment of political rights and a stake in society. Because of this, there are many Africans who, today, tend to equate freedom with communism.'

In the 1980s, with communists still prominent in the hierarchy of both the ANC and Umkhonto, government ministers sought ways to divide the 'nationalists' within the ANC from the communists. They tried the same approach with Mandela in prison, but his response was the same as it had been in 1964. 'Co-operation between the ANC and SACP goes back to the early twenties and has always been, and still is, strictly limited to the struggle against racial oppression and for a just society,' he wrote in his memorandum in 1989. 'At no time has the organisation ever adopted, or co-operated with, communism itself.' He went on: 'No dedicated ANC member will ever heed the call to break with the SACP. We regard such a demand as a purely divisive government strategy. It is in fact a call on us to commit suicide. Which man of honour will ever desert a life-long friend at the insistence of a common opponent and still retain a measure of credibility among his people? Which opponent will ever trust such a treacherous freedom fighter? Yet this is what the government is, in effect, asking us to do: to desert our faithful allies. We will not fall into that trap.'

Botha's view of the ANC was not shared in other parts of the white establishment. Watching in despair the unending cycle of black revolt, government repression and international sanctions, the white business community had become increasingly outspoken in its condemnation of the government's failure to introduce meaningful reform and resolved to take its own initiative. In 1986 a group of influential businessmen, led by the chairman of the giant Anglo-American Corporation, Gavin Relly, flew to Lusaka for talks with ANC leaders. The meeting was a curious affair, a group of tycoons and revolutionaries sitting down side by side at a presidential lodge in a game park, the blacks dressed impeccably in suits and ties, the whites wearing more casual attire, looking almost unkempt by comparison, everyone in a friendly mood discussing in good humour the rival virtues of capitalism and socialism. But the message was unmistakable: discussions between the two sides were worthwhile. Other groups – opposition politicians, churchmen, students – soon found their way to Lusaka. In private, senior members of the Broederbond made their own contacts with the ANC.

Botha's response was to denounce the businessmen for their 'disloyalty' and for showing 'signs of weakness towards the enemies of South Africa' and he did his best to obstruct further contacts. A group of respected Dutch Reformed Church clergymen who wanted to talk to the ANC he branded as 'naïve' and 'childish' and threatened to confiscate their passports. De Klerk took the same view about contacts with the ANC, and he frequently clashed over the matter with his brother, Willem de Klerk, a prominent Afrikaner journalist and intellectual, who held regular discussions with ANC officials in exile.

'No matter how well-intentioned these talks may be,' said de Klerk in October 1989, 'the result is, generally, that the ANC and others exploit them to mask the intrinsic nature of revolutionary organisations and to promote an undeserved image of reasonableness. Thus participants in such talks are playing into the hands of forces that are still set on destabilising South Africa and destroying law and order.'

De Klerk's dilemma, however, was that once he had decided that negotiations for a new dispensation were inevitable, there was no way of starting them without the inclusion of the ANC. No credible African leader, not even conservative homeland leaders, was prepared to negotiate with the government until Mandela was released and the ban on the ANC was lifted. But the risks for de Klerk in doing so were considerable. The government had devoted years of propaganda to telling South Africa's whites that the ANC was a bunch of communist terrorists. It had repeatedly committed itself not to negotiate with any leader or organisation that was engaged in violence. By abandoning this position, it was conceding a significant victory to the ANC. The result might be further violence as black radicals took to the streets to push the revolution forwards. In any event, de Klerk was bound to undermine his support within the white community and boost the threat from right-wing whites which he constantly feared.

On the other hand, de Klerk reasoned, there would be considerable advantage in seizing the initiative and capturing 'high moral ground'. The collapse of socialist governments in Eastern Europe in 1989 had not only deprived the ANC of one of its main sources of financial, logistical and military support, but undermined its whole ideological strategy. Moreover, it meant that communist support in neighbouring territories would be substantially reduced. With the withdrawal of Cuban troops from Angola and the declining Soviet interest in the region, the threat of 'total onslaught' was rapidly receding. 'We recognised it as a unique opportunity in the course of history, a God-given opportunity – we thought of it very much in Christian terms – to ensure that conflict in South Africa could be resolved,' recalled de Klerk's principal strategist, Gerrit Viljoen. The chances were that the ANC, poorly organised and ill-prepared for peace, would fall into disarray, leaving the government to forge ahead with a new alliance with conservative black organisations. Even the mythic status surrounding Mandela might evaporate once he was released. Whatever actions the government decided upon in lifting restrictions on political activity, could be carried out in careful stages. In any event the government would always remain firmly in control.

To prepare the ground, de Klerk arranged to meet Mandela at the Tuynhuys, the president's office in Cape Town in December 1989. The meeting went well. 'We immediately started talking freely to each other,' de Klerk recalled. Mandela was impressed: 'He met me on the basis of equality and discussed issues objectively.' Further meetings followed. But Mandela remained sceptical about de Klerk's real intentions.

Few people anticipated that de Klerk would finally take such sweeping measures. Before parliament on 2 February 1990, he announced not only that Mandela would be released but that the ban on the African National Congress and even the South African Communist Party and the radical Pan-Africanist Congress would be lifted. Emergency regulations would be eased; media restrictions would be abolished; and political prisoners would be released. 'It is time for us to break out of the cycle of violence and break through to peace and reconciliation.' He outlined new aims towards which the government would work. These included: a new democratic constitution; universal franchise; no domination; the protection of minorities as well as of individual rights; and a sound economy 'based on proven economic principles and private enterprise'. He asked black leaders to join him: 'The time for negotiation has come.'

The boldness of de Klerk's reforms set South Africa

on to an entirely new course. In effect, he had pronounced the death sentence of apartheid. The central issue had always been political power. None of the reforms hitherto implemented by Nationalist leaders had come close to addressing that issue. Now, in a stroke, de Klerk had conceded one person one vote and opened the way for its attainment. The legacies of apartheid would endure for many years. The whites could be expected to defend their heritage with every vigour. The transition to majority rule involved many perils. But there was now no going back.

Nine days later, on 11 February 1990, Mandela walked to freedom through the gates of Victor Verster jail, hand in hand with his wife, Winnie, to meet a waiting crowd of supporters and the ranks of the world's media. Tall, strikingly elegant, with creases and furrows etched on his face, and a slightly fragile air, he greeted the crowd with a clenched fist salute, then turned and walked back to his car before leaving at the head of a cavalcade for Cape Town. As daylight was fading, he appeared on the balcony of City Hall, overlooking the Grand Parade packed with 100,000 people. Twenty-seven years of imprisonment had done nothing to diminish his commitment to the cause. The struggle against apartheid had to be intensified on all fronts, he said. He called for mass action and the continuation of 'armed struggle' and international economic sanctions. 'We express the hope that a climate conducive to a negotiated settlement will be created soon so that there may no longer be the need for the armed struggle.' But he also paid tribute to de Klerk as 'a man of integrity' who had gone further than any other Nationalist president in taking 'real steps to normalise the situation'. And he concluded by quoting his words at his trial in 1964 which, he said, were 'as true today as they were then'.

'During my lifetime I have dedicated myself to this struggle of the African people. I have fought against black domination and I have fought against white domination. I have cherished the ideal of a democratic and free society in which all persons live together in harmony and with equal opportunities. It is an ideal which I hope to live for and achieve. But if needs be it is an ideal for which I am prepared to die.'

Chapter 3

The Road to Negotiations

In fits and starts, de Klerk proceeded with the business of dismantling apartheid laws. One by one, the pillars of apartheid came down: the Land Acts which gave whites exclusive use of 87 per cent of South African land; the Group Areas Act which demarcated separate residential areas for each racial group; the Separate Amenities Act which provided separate facilities in all spheres of public life (separate buses, trains, post offices, restaurants and theatres); and finally the Population Registration Act which classified people by race and which constituted the foundation for all other apartheid laws. 'We shall never be able to have complete peace in South Africa as long as there is statutory discrimination,' de Klerk told parliament.

He also conceded the failure of the black homelands system and the need for their eventual reintegration into South Africa. The homelands policy had been designed to strip Africans of any claim to South African citizenship and hence a political voice. Every African was deemed to be a citizen of one of ten tribal homelands, even though millions had no connections there. The geography of the homelands made little sense. Most were made up from scattered and fragmented pieces of land: KwaZulu originally consisted of 48 pieces of land and scores of smaller tracts, and Bophuthatswana of 19 major pieces of land spread across three of South Africa's provinces. Ciskei consisted of 15 pieces of land, Lebowa of 14,

Gazankulu of four, and Venda, KaNgwane and Transkei of three each. Only one homeland, Qwa Qwa, an area of about 200 square miles, consisted of a single contiguous territory. In an attempt to make the homelands ethnically purer, the government had resorted to large-scale removals, adding thousands more victims to the population upheavals which apartheid had already caused. In all, more than three million people were uprooted to satisfy the requirements of apartheid.

For an élite group of African politicians, chiefs, civil servants and traders, self-government and 'independence' for the homelands brought substantial rewards. Cabinet ministers, members of legislative assemblies and civil servants gained increasingly from high salaries, loans, land and housing, as the South African authorities sought to establish a prosperous middle class which would underpin the homelands system and provide them with allies in the business of government. Modern towns appeared in Mmabatho, Ulundi, Umtata, Bisho and other homeland capitals. But the homelands themselves remained decaying backwaters, populated by an impoverished peasantry and dependent on handouts from Pretoria and remittances from migrant labour. They became a byword for corruption, poverty and human rights' abuses, and a source of increasing embarrassment. By 1990, three of the four 'independent' homelands, Ciskei, Transkei and Venda, were ruled by military dictators and the fourth, Bophuthatswana, had had to be rescued by South African troops from an attempted coup.

De Klerk also abandoned his belief in the merits of group-based politics. In 1990 the National Party opened its ranks to all races for the first time since its formation in 1914 and began to extol the virtues of liberal democracy. In view of its record, there was little likelihood of a dramatic demand for membership. But opinion polls amongst blacks nevertheless suggested that de Klerk's personal popularity was fast rising. Paying his first official visit to Soweto, the sprawling black city south-east of Johannesburg, 'Comrade FW' was given a noticeably warm welcome.

In his dealings with Mandela and the ANC, too, de Klerk managed to strike up a good working relationship. When the government and the ANC finally sat down together at the president's official residence in Cape Town in May 1990 – for the first time since the ANC's formation in 1912 – the atmosphere was relatively cordial. 'Within a matter of minutes,' remarked a senior ANC official, 'everybody understood that there was nobody in the room with horns.' Much was made of the personal 'chemistry' between de Klerk and Mandela. 'I find him to be an honest person, very capable and a strong leader,' remarked Mandela about de Klerk. 'He is sincere in his efforts to bring about fundamental political changes in the country.' There were disputes over the return of exiles and the release of political prisoners but by August 1990 sufficient progress had been made for the ANC formally to agree to suspend all armed action.

For the ANC, the business of converting itself from a liberation movement into a political organisation was a far more difficult process. De Klerk's announcement in February 1990 had caught it by surprise. The ANC's strategy for years had been based on plans for a revolutionary seizure of power, not on the possibility of peaceful negotiation. Trained guerrillas brought up on songs about how Umkhonto would march across the Limpopo to take Pretoria by storm now found themselves returning through Jan Smuts airport near Johannesburg, pushing trolleys. Many activists in the townships were reluctant to forgo the prospect of revolution and resented the ease with which ANC leaders appeared to settle into confidential talks with the white government and agreed to suspend armed struggle.

In exile, despite the disputes and divisions which had surfaced, the ANC had managed to hold itself together as an omnibus movement in which every shade of opinion, from liberal democrat to hardline communist, was represented. Now there were new tensions as different generations of leadership asserted themselves: the elderly veterans of the 1950s, like Mandela, emerging from years of imprisonment; the Soweto generation of the 1970s returning from exile as guerrilla commissars; and the radical young leaders of the 1980s internal revolt. In exile, the ANC was used to acting as a secretive, authoritarian organisation with military personnel prominent in its hierarchy. Decisions had been taken by a revolutionary council and passed down the chain of command. The covert nature of operations meant that there had been little room for dissent. Those who opposed the party line were more than likely to be accused of being collaborators. Now the ANC faced a bewildering variety of party branches, community organisations, youth groups and trade union affiliates, all demanding a say. In exile, the ANC's headquarters was a cramped, single-storey building off an alleyway in downtown Lusaka, where it gained a reputation for chronic inefficiency. Now it needed to establish hundreds of party offices, organise the return of 40,000 exiles, ensure the welfare of returning guerrillas, devise new negotiating strategies, raise funds, weld a massive, restless constituency into a coherent political force and deal with a government seeking to place it at a disadvantage at every stage. The result, more often than not, was organisational chaos. Blunders were commonplace. Criticism was rife. As Mandela noted ruefully in his concluding remarks at an ANC 'consultative' conference in December 1990: 'One of the most disappointing features of the conference was that there was hardly a word of praise.' Mandela himself faced charges from the disgruntled rank and file of élitism, secrecy and lack of accountability. The ANC's national conference – the first in three decades – had to be postponed for six months, so great was the disorder. When it was eventually held in July 1991, many of the same criticisms were still heard. A confidential internal report presented to the conference noted: 'We lack enterprise, creativity and initiative. We appear very happy to remain pigeon-holed within the confines of populist rhetoric and clichés... Clearly we have not utilised our full potential to mobilise millions of our people into effective action.'

Watching from the sidelines, the far right was enraged by the whole process. De Klerk was denounced as a traitor, a sell-out: 'The only leader in the Western world who is negotiating himself, his party and his people out of power,' railed the Conservative Party leader, Andries Treurnicht. Treurnicht, an elderly ideologue wedded to ideas of racial purity and power, and a former *predikant* and newspaper editor, was the true heir to Hendrik Verwoerd. What he advocated was absolute apartheid, a geographical separation between the races. A former cabinet minister, Treurnicht had broken away to form the Conservative Party in 1982 when Botha had introduced his plan to offer a role in parliament to the Coloured and Indian communities. 'Any attempt at multi-racialism, especially in government, must of necessity lead to a never-ending conflict between the race groups,' claimed Treurnicht. The Conservative Party attracted increasing white support from blue-collar workers in mining and manufacturing, from low-level civil servants, office clerks, small farmers, and from the mostly Afrikaner police force, and, in general, from those more directly threatened by the prospect of black advancement. In the 1989 election, the Conservative Party gained 31 per cent of the white vote, and increased the number of its seats from 23 to 39.

In the wake of *Rooivrydag*, Red Friday, as the day of de Klerk's groundbreaking announcements in February 1990 was known in far-right circles, Treurnicht's objective became the establishment of an independent white state – an Afrikaner *volkstaat*. He offered no suggestion about what its borders might be, nor about how it might be brought about: there was not a single magisterial district in South Africa where whites, let alone Afrikaners, actually constituted a majority of inhabitants. But it was an idea with immense appeal in the Conservative Party as well as among other factions on the far right. 'We in the Conservative Party are adamant that there is a territory which belongs historically and otherwise to the white nation,' said Treurnicht. 'While we accept that there are whites who are prepared to live under an ANC government in a unitary state, there are others – we believe, the majority – who will never submit themselves to a communist terrorist regime... Unless any future constitutional dispensation addresses the problems of ethnicity and self-determination, it will be a waste of time and a recipe for discord.'

To rally support for this new cause and to demonstrate the strength of the far right, Treurnicht organised a mass meeting in May 1990 at the Voortrekker Monument, a massive granite temple built on the heights overlooking Pretoria to commemorate the deeds of the Boer trekkers who broke away from British rule in 1836 to found their own republic. All the paraphernalia of the far right were on display: the horses, wagons, guns and flags – symbols they cherished as representing the valiant stand of whites in the laager battling against a black onslaught. Horsemen in khaki uniforms from the Afrikaner Weerstandsbeweging, the Afrikaner Resistance Movement (AWB), paraded their swastika-like banners and proudly brandished pistols. Before a crowd of 60,000 whites, Treurnicht pledged 'a third freedom struggle' in pursuit of Afrikaner self-determination, alluding to the possibility of resistance similar to that of the Boers in the two wars against British imperial rule in the nineteenth century. 'You do not have enough jails to keep Afrikaner nationalism imprisoned,' he declared. 'We warn: this is an unfair government which no longer represents the *volk*.'

Treurnicht's Conservative Party represented the respectable face of the far right. Other groups, like the AWB, advocated outright violence. An overtly fascist organisation, using Nazi-style ritual and insignia, its aim was to restore the nineteenth-century Boer republics crushed by the British army. Led by Eugene Terre'Blanche, a former policeman known for powerful oratory and a bombastic manner, the AWB was the moving force behind the formation of scores of 'commando' units. 'We refuse to be put under an ANC government,' declared Terre'Blanche. 'That night there will be war in South Africa ... we will fight, as our forefathers fought, until we have won.' In one town after another, white vigilante groups sprang up 'to protect white property, women and children against blacks'.

The potential for racial conflict was clear enough. The gold-mining town of Welkom in the Orange Free State was among the first to arm itself against the *swart gevaar* – the 'black peril'. Organised groups of white vigilantes began to cruise Welkom's streets at night, carrying automatic rifles, pump-action shotguns and pistols. The local vigilante group, Blanke Veiligheidswag (White Security Guard), which had 3,000 members, claimed that its men were there only to protect life and property, to fill a vacuum which they said had resulted from a collapse in local policing. Leaders of local black organisations asserted that they were beating up any black person found on the streets after dark. When two blacks were killed by vigilantes in May, the black community called a consumer boycott of white-owned shops. White vigilante patrols increased. At the mine site, a mob of angry black miners demonstrated against the white foremen who, they claimed, had been harassing them for wearing ANC badges. Mine security guards fired on them with tear-gas and birdshot. In the ensuing battle, two whites were stoned and stabbed to death. Army and police reinforcements were rushed to the town. In a deal made with government representatives, the Welkom vigilante leader agreed to keep his men off the streets in exchange for more police protection and a promise that the government would try to persuade black leaders to give up the boycott. A few days later, a rally in the township resolved to stop the boycott. But as people walked home from the rally, youths and police clashed in a battle which left 13 blacks dead and more than 100 injured.

Along with vigilante action came a spate of bomb attacks. The targets included government offices, a radical Afrikaans newspaper and a war museum in Pretoria where the peace treaty ending the Anglo-Boer war had been signed. A bomb explosion during the rush hour in Johannesburg injured 27 people, most of them women. There was also an upsurge in racial attacks, notably 'drive-by' shootings. But terrorist activity mounted by the far right never posed a serious threat, despite the wild rhetoric of its leaders. And it was soon overshadowed by a far greater danger emerging from the green rolling hills of Natal where a vicious struggle for power had developed. It centred on the controversial leader of the KwaZulu homeland, Mangosuthu Buthelezi.

Buthelezi's role in the apartheid system was a complex one. In his youth he was marked down by the authorities as a troublemaker. While studying at Fort Hare University, from where he was expelled in his final year for taking part in a political protest, he joined the Youth League of the African National Congress; among those whom he openly admired were Nelson Mandela and Chief Luthuli, a former ANC president who had been awarded the Nobel Peace Prize in 1961. Buthelezi was nevertheless prepared to work within the apartheid system. 'If we can get all these human rights and dignities through separate development,' he said in 1970, 'well, let's get on with it.' Elected as Chief Executive Officer of the KwaZulu Territorial Authority in 1970 and as Chief Minister in 1976, he developed the art of opposing Pretoria's homelands policy while at the same time playing a leading role in it. Co-operation was justified, he argued, on pragmatic grounds. The homelands policy enabled Zulus to acquire vital administrative experience which they would be able to use to good effect in a multiracial South Africa in the future and it provided them, too, with a platform from which to oppose apartheid.

Using his position as a member of the Zulu royal family, Buthelezi built up a powerful cultural and political movement, Inkatha ye Nkululeko we Sizwe (Freedom of the Nation), which gained support not only in KwaZulu but in urban areas as well. Within a few years, Inkatha claimed to have 350,000 paid-up members, making it the largest black political organisation allowed to function in South Africa's history. Buthelezi himself, according to some opinion polls, was regarded by many Africans as a more important national leader than Mandela. In 1978 he won the first election in KwaZulu with nearly a clean sweep of the seats. As head of the KwaZulu government, he possessed considerable powers of patronage and control and used them ruthlessly. In many respects he resembled a tribal potentate, intolerant of criticism, brooking no opposition, given to making interminable speeches, and constantly reminiscing about the past exploits of the Zulu people. In sum, he seemed an ideal partner for the government. But having lent the homelands system greater credibility than any other homeland leader, he then delivered it a crippling blow by refusing independence.

The set-back for Pretoria was severe. Two homelands had already taken independence: Transkei in 1976, and Bophuthatswana in 1977. In theory, the African population of South Africa had been reduced by 3.4 million people. The Minister of Bantu Affairs and Development, Connie Mulder, exulted at the time: 'If our policy is taken to its full logical conclusion as far as the black people are concerned, there will not be one black man with South African citizenship.' Though two more homelands, Venda and Ciskei, eventually were to choose independence, Buthelezi's refusal to do so effectively ruined the government's plans.

Initially he remained on good terms with the exiled leaders of the ANC. When the Inkatha movement was launched in the 1970s, the ANC saw it as a vehicle which could advance, rather than retard, the cause of liberation and sought to influence its activities from abroad. The ANC also approved his assuming power in KwaZulu as homeland leader. But the relationship soon ended acrimoniously, with the ANC accusing Buthelezi of building Inkatha into 'a personal power base' and Buthelezi accusing the ANC of trying to hijack Inkatha for its own ends. During the 1980s the feud became increasingly bitter. Buthelezi vociferously opposed violence, sanctions and disinvestment and paid short shrift to any criticism. In a letter to the ANC's exiled leader, Oliver Tambo, in 1984, he wrote: 'In this part of South Africa, we come from warrior stock and there is a resilient determination in KwaZulu and in Inkatha which even the full might of the state will never be able to flatten. Do your colleagues really think they can flatten us on the way to their envisaged victory?' From Lusaka, as the townships revolt got underway in the mid-1980s, the ANC denounced Buthelezi as 'a counter-revolutionary', 'a puppet', and 'a snake poisoning the people of South Africa (which) needs to be hit on the head'.

The maverick role that Buthelezi played involved high risks. Though he tried to distance himself from Botha's regime, his following began to fall away. One opinion poll showed that between 1977 and 1988 Inkatha's support in the industrial heartland of South Africa – the Pretoria-Witwatersrand-Vaal (PWV) area – declined from more than 30 per cent to less than five per cent. Even worse, there were clear signs that Inkatha's support in its home base of KwaZulu/Natal was rapidly eroding, notably among urban blacks. Pro-ANC youth groups and trade unions were becoming increasingly active. In 1987 Inkatha embarked on a recruitment drive.

The ugly contest that followed engulfed KwaZulu/Natal in bouts of violence for years to come. Inkatha possessed considerable advantages. It was a well-organised political movement with a clear hierarchy and chain of command, able to hold regular public meetings and rallies. It drew its support from the Zulu establishment, from chiefs, councillors, elected legislative assembly members, indunas, businessmen, civil servants and other government employees. To attract workers, it had established a trade union wing in 1985, Uwusa (United Workers' Union of South Africa), enabling it to compete with the pro-ANC trade union alliance, Cosatu (Congress of South African Trade Unions). Above all, it could count on the support of the KwaZulu Police (KZP) which had been established in 1980 and which Buthelezi, as Minister of Police, had turned into a formidable paramilitary force. In addition to regular policemen, special 'kitskonstabels' were recruited, mainly from the ranks of Inkatha, some with criminal records. They were given limited training, then sent back to their communities, armed with pump-action shotguns.

The task of taking on pro-ANC supporters was given official encouragement from Pretoria. At a police ceremony in Pietermaritzburg in 1988, the Minister of Law and Order, Adriaan Vlok, declared: 'The police intend to face the future with moderates and fight against radical groups ... Radicals, who are trying to destroy South Africa, will not be tolerated. We will fight them. We have put our foot in that direction, and we will eventually win the Pietermaritzburg area.'

Buthelezi's strategy was to appeal to Zulu pride and sense of martial tradition and to assert the notion that the Zulu people and Inkatha were synonymous. Zulus, he said, were a 'mighty nation' with a 'glorious heritage' who needed to stand together in the face of enemies who did not 'want the Zulu nation to unite'. He liked to recount how he had learnt politics at his mother's lap listening to tales of Zulu resistance to British settlers in the nineteenth century and how his great-grandfather, Cetshwayo, had routed the British army at the battle of Isandhlwana in 1879. In public he appeared frequently in traditional Zulu dress, draping a leopard skin across his shoulders and holding a shield, a stick and gleaming spear in his hands.

His opponents in Natal were Zulus from the ranks of urban blacks, from community groups, the landless, unemployed and, above all, the youth, all struggling for survival in crowded shack settlements and townships and resentful of the power and patronage enjoyed by the Zulu establishment. The numbers of this constituency were forever swelling. Between 1979 and 1989, the population of greater Durban more than trebled from under one million to three million.

The conflict became essentially territorial. Inkatha leaders, usually known as 'warlords', formed armed groups – 'impis' – to drive out opponents. Radical groups responded in kind. Police were frequently accused of collusion in Inkatha attacks, of harassing radical groups but failing to deal with the activities of warlords and known killers and of standing by while the impis went to work. Attackers were sometimes transported, heavily armed, in buses in broad daylight. Assassinations were commonplace; massacres were perpetrated. Many areas became 'no-go' areas for one side or the other. Mixed in with political rivalry were the activities of criminal gangs and violent disputes over land, water and housing. By 1990, more than 3,000 people had been killed.

The unbanning of the ANC in 1990, unleashing a wave of political activity across South Africa, presented new threats to Buthelezi. In protest against the violence in KwaZulu/Natal, the ANC and its trade union affiliate, Cosatu, organised an 'isolate Buthelezi' campaign which, on July 2, brought three million workers out on a 'stayaway', closing most factories in Natal. Inkatha was proclaimed 'an enemy of the people'. In the Transvaal townships, the houses of many Inkatha officials, notably township councillors, were petrol-bombed. A few weeks later, Buthelezi took his own initiative. He turned Inkatha into a fully-fledged political party, the Inkatha Freedom Party (IFP), opened it to all races, and launched a recruitment campaign in Transvaal, concentrating on township hostels along the Reef. What followed became known as the 'Reef township war', bringing a level of violence to South Africa never witnessed before.

The hostels were a natural recruiting ground for Inkatha. More than 50 hostels in townships in the East Rand and West Rand were occupied mainly by Zulu-speaking workers from rural areas of KwaZulu and Natal who had come to the Reef in search of work. The conditions in which they lived were appalling. The hostels were generally overcrowded, squalid and insanitary blocks providing only rudimentary facilities. Township residents tended to sneer at people who lived there. But for the occupants they offered a vital base from which to earn a living. Coming mostly from a traditional rural background, they tended to resent the undisciplined behaviour of township youths. They were notably hostile to the coercive tactics used by radical groups in the townships to enforce boycotts, stayaways and other forms of anti-apartheid protest. The only reason hostel dwellers endured such grim places was to work and earn money for their families in rural areas, for most homesteads in rural Zululand were dependent on remittances from migrants in Johannesburg. There were also particular fears about demands, made by local ANC leaders at public rallies, that hostel dwellers should vacate hostels to make way for returning exiles who needed a home, and about suggestions that hostels should be upgraded to family units, which might also have led to single migrants being thrown out. Inkatha officials exploited these fears, warning hostel residents that they were in danger of losing their 'homes', as a means of gaining support. Aggravating all this was the ethnic factor. For years, permanent residents and hostel dwellers, whether of Zulu, Xhosa or mixed origin, had lived together peaceably. But Inkatha now used Zulu allegiance as the basis for its recruitment campaign. Its adversaries in the squatter settlements surrounding the hostels were often Xhosas supporting the ANC. Ethnic tensions rapidly mounted. Rumours abounded of imminent attack by Zulu or by Xhosa fighters.

On July 22, the Reef War broke out. It started in Sebokeng in a battle between residents and hostel dwellers which flared up shortly after an Inkatha rally and then spread from one township to another as hostel dwellers launched attacks on nearby squatter settlements and residential areas, setting off endless cycles of revenge and retaliation. Within days several hundred were dead. Zulu hostel dwellers expelled Xhosa-speakers and other non-Zulus from hostels, turning them into Zulu fortresses. Zulu families in the surrounding areas, facing persecution, sought protection there. As communities split, Zulus came to be identified as Inkatha supporters and Xhosas as ANC supporters, regardless of their real allegiances. Many Zulu-speakers living near hostels were forced to align themselves with hostel dwellers as their only means of defence against revenge attacks by township residents. Thousands abandoned their shacks and homes to escape the violence. Some townships became divided into rival territories with large 'no-go' areas of wrecked and deserted houses separating them. In August, 500 people died over an eleven-day period.

The role of the police, as in Natal, became increasingly controversial. Police refused to disarm Zulu impis of their spears, axes, knives, sticks and iron bars, on the grounds that these were traditional weapons that Zulus were entitled to carry. They were also accused of standing by while hostel dwellers launched their murderous raids into surrounding territory or of actually assisting them. There had been a long history of brutal conflict between police and radical groups in the townships. The two sides had, in effect, been at war since the Soweto revolt of 1976. To many in the police, the ANC was still 'the enemy', and a justifiable target for Inkatha supporters. But the suspicion soon grew that something more sinister was happening. In September, 26 people died and more than 100 were injured when a six-man gang ran through a Johannesburg commuter train shooting passengers at random; a second gang, lying in wait on a station platform attacked survivors trying to escape from the train. The attack had all the hallmarks of the kind of terrorist activity carried out for years in Mozambique by rebels trained and supported by South African military intelligence.

All this coincided with a wave of public disclosures about dirty tricks operations conducted by police and army units in the 1970s and 1980s in their campaign against the ANC and other government opponents. In October 1989, a black policeman, under sentence of death for the murder of a white farmer, earned a stay of execution by claiming that he had been a member of a security police assassination squad set up to eliminate government opponents and identified its commander as Captain Dirk Coetzee. The following month, Coetzee, having fled the country, admitted his involvement with assassination squads from 1976 to 1981 and related a series of murders, abductions and bomb attacks carried out in neighbouring countries and in Europe. He claimed that assassination squads were still at work. In March 1990, an official inquiry (the Harms Commission) into the conduct of security forces, which de Klerk eventually agreed to set up, was told of similar activity at home and abroad carried out by a defence force covert unit known as the Civil Co-operation Bureau (CCB), established in 1985. The unit was still active, with an annual budget of R28 million. The verdict of the inquiry was that the CCB operated as a law unto itself and had its own political agenda. Its actions had 'contaminated the whole security arm of the state'. In July 1990, the government announced the unit would be disbanded.

With all this evidence of security force involvement in murder and dirty tricks at hand, it seemed all the more plausible, in the wake of several train massacres and attacks on squatter settlements, to suspect a conspiracy of right-wing elements in the military and the police to wreck the negotiation process. Meeting in September, de Klerk and Mandela agreed that there was a 'third force' or 'hidden hand' at work. De Klerk's dilemma was how to purge right-wing extremists from the ranks of the security forces upon which he relied to maintain law and order during the turbulent transition from apartheid. Soon after taking office, he had dispensed with the elaborate system of national security management which Botha had constructed as part of his 'total strategy' to meet 'total onslaught'. But key personnel, wedded to that strategy, were still in place. They believed the 'enemy' was still the ANC and acted accordingly. They had also become accustomed to operating autonomously. As the Harms inquiry noted, the CCB had ignored requests from the President, the Minister of Defence and the Chief of the Defence Force. 'Requests by parliament, the Auditor-General and the commission were treated with contempt.'

For month after month the clashes continued, with varying degrees of intensity. Police action to stamp out the violence merely curbed it temporarily. Political efforts to solve it proved fruitless. A meeting between Mandela and Buthelezi, their first encounter in 28 years, which finally took place in January 1991, produced fine words about peace. But within weeks, hundreds more had died. The ANC blamed the government. The government blamed the ANC and Inkatha. Inkatha and the ANC each blamed the police for supporting the opposing faction. The police still refused to disarm Zulus carrying 'traditional' weapons. In despair, the South African Council of Churches said it had reached the conclusion that the leaders of the factions involved in township violence were 'impotent to halt the carnage'. In May, after an episode in which a thousand Inkatha supporters armed with spears, automatic rifles and pangas hacked their way through a squatter community outside Kagiso township on the West Rand, Mandela declared it was time for de Klerk to stand up to Buthelezi. Later that month, when the ANC boycotted a government-sponsored conference called to try to end the violence, de Klerk accused it of 'playing politics' while parts of the country were left 'ankle-deep in blood'.

The evidence of security force involvement in the mayhem, meanwhile, steadily mounted. Press investigations revealed that 200 Inkatha hit-men had been trained by South African military intelligence in the Caprivi Strip in 1986, before being deployed in Natal and the Transvaal. Buthelezi confirmed the training, but said the men had been attached to KwaZulu officials to act as bodyguards. A former army sergeant alleged that a special forces unit had been involved in train massacres and a string of other incidents. In June 1991, a former military intelligence officer claimed that the army was fully involved in the funding and supply of weapons to Inkatha with the aim of fanning violence in the townships and weakening the ANC. A defence force spokesman dismissed the allegations as 'ridiculous'. The following month, in what became known as 'Inkathagate', the government was forced to admit that it had secretly channelled funds to Inkatha and to its affiliated trade union, Uwusa. Government funding for Uwusa had been going on since its establishment six years previously; in the case of Inkatha, the security police had paid funds to help it organise political rallies to shore up support for Buthelezi.

The disclosures were a humiliation for de Klerk. They called into question his good faith in negotiating with the ANC and seriously weakened the government's credibility at home and abroad. No longer did de Klerk's denials that he was pursuing a 'double agenda' – talking to the ANC while at the same time supporting the violent activities of its opponents – carry much weight. Buthelezi's reputation also suffered: for all his claims of independent leadership, he was shown up as a weakling, relying on hand-outs from Pretoria's security police to keep up his support. Inkatha, claimed Mandela, had 'permitted itself to become an extension of the Pretoria regime, its instrument and surrogate'. For Mandela, too, the disclosures caused considerable embarrassment, providing ammunition for his radical critics in the ANC who had repeatedly warned that he was placing too much trust in de Klerk and the government. Mandela was deeply shocked by the cavalier way in which de Klerk tried to gloss over the scandal and continued to dismiss his complaints about security force involvement in 'third force' activity. 'We believed', he said, 'that President de Klerk was a man of integrity. But subsequent events have shown that perhaps we were hasty and that there was a little bit of naïvety on our part because he has turned out to be a totally different man from what he was initially.' However, he went on, it was irrelevant whether or not de Klerk was a man of integrity. 'What is clear is that the violence that is raging in the country suits his purposes.'

Eighteen months after de Klerk had announced his bold reforms, South Africa was a country in the hands of a discredited government, afflicted by appalling bouts of violence, no nearer the start of negotiations, with distrust manifest on all sides, plagued by right-wing acts of terrorism and mired in economic recession.

But there was within South Africa an even deeper malaise. A culture of violence had developed amongst successive generations of black youths. They had been at the forefront of the Soweto uprising of the 1970s, the townships revolt of the 1980s, and the political struggles of the 1990s. At each stage the use of violence had become more widespread and more extreme. Not only was it now endemic; there were signs that it was accelerating beyond control.

The Soweto uprising of 1976 had been 'a children's war'. It had started as a result of student protest against conditions in black schools and it became the most serious challenge the government had yet faced. The system of Bantu Education, as it was then known, had been designed by Verwoerd to educate Africans sufficiently to serve the labour needs of the white economy but not beyond. 'There is no place for him in the European community above the level of certain forms of labour,' Verwoerd decreed in 1953. The system had produced a legacy of inferior schooling, poorly-trained teachers, overcrowded classrooms and inadequate equipment. Because of deliberate restrictions on places in middle and higher schools, hundreds of thousands of children – 'push-outs', as they were known – left school with no greater prospects than menial work or unemployment. Even matriculants completing secondary school were then blocked by a whole range of apartheid restrictions affecting the kind of employment for which they could apply. When the Department of Bantu Education tried to enforce a ruling about the teaching of Afrikaans in schools, students went on strike. A peaceful protest march was stopped by police with gunfire. The ensuing revolt spread to schools across the country, lasting several months. Even though student violence was eventually repressed, protests against 'gutter education' continued. The school system was constantly disrupted by boycotts.

The townships revolt, starting in 1984, was sporadic at first, ignited by local grievances, flaring up with great intensity, shifting from one area to the next and gradually drawing in more and more of an urban population that was alienated, deprived and hostile. At the forefront were groups of black youths – 'comrades' as they came to be known – determined to destroy 'the system' and ready to defy armed police and soldiers in the dusty and decrepit streets of the townships with stones, catapults and petrol bombs. Many saw themselves as the shock troops of the revolution and believed that it was within their reach. Students joined the fray, forsaking their classrooms once more. 'Liberation before education' became their slogan. Urged on by the ANC in exile to mount 'a people's war' and make the townships 'ungovernable', young comrades enforced consumer boycotts, organised rent strikes, attacked government buildings, set up 'people's courts' and hunted down 'collaborators' – town councillors, local policemen and others deemed to support 'the system'. Their trademark became the 'necklace' method of killing – a tyre filled with petrol, thrown over a victim and set on fire. Such methods were endorsed by radical leaders like Mandela's wife, Winnie: 'Together, hand-in-hand, with our boxes of matches and our necklaces, we shall liberate this country,' she told them. The comrades – some as young as ten years old – also faced the brunt of security force repression. Hundreds were killed; thousands were arrested, many of whom were subsequently maltreated and tortured, returning to the townships all the more embittered and hostile. By the time the revolt had been put down in 1986, a whole generation of black youth had been brutalised. Their schooling had been disrupted for more than a decade. They became known as 'the lost generation'. But they were also a generation which had experienced raw power. And this experience would not be forgotten easily.

In the 1990s, the same atmosphere of revolutionary fervour prevailed. Mandela, emerging from Victor Verster prison, declared the need for armed struggle to continue. For months on end, as the ANC endeavoured to bolster its standing in confronting the government, the rhetoric of armed struggle was used, giving township activists licence to pursue opponents at will. Their targets were once again township councillors supporting Inkatha and local police. In the first seven months of 1990, more than 400 attacks on black councillors and police were recorded. Necklace executions once again became common. Guns; in particular AK47s, were now readily available, many smuggled in from Mozambique and Angola. The Reef War added a new dimension. In response to the ferocious attacks organised by hostel dwellers, young comrades in surrounding residential areas and squatter camps set up self-defence units (SDUs) with the help of Umkhonto. Some SDUs succeeded in offering protection to local communities, but others waged an often indiscriminate war of retribution on hostel dwellers, widening the cycle of violence. Some broke up into factions and engaged in their own form of territorial warfare; others were taken over by criminal gangs, becoming notorious for extortion, rape and murder, and adding to the spiralling volume of violent crime. All lacked political control. At the base of this anarchic activity was a vast underclass of youth roaming the streets – unskilled, unemployed, undisciplined, fed on revolutionary slogans, but now angry and resentful of how little the revolution had brought them.

Such was the scale of disorder that it brought together rival politicians fearing descent into chaos. In September 1991, a National Peace Accord was signed by the government, the ANC, Inkatha, homeland leaders and a variety of religious, business and trade union organisations. The accord provided for codes of conduct by political parties and police; a network of peace monitors and enforcement mechanisms to help resolve conflict at local and regional levels; and an independent judicial commission to investigate and expose causes of violence. There was considerable scepticism about what impact the peace accord would have. Indeed, in October, South Africa experienced one of its worst months of violence on record. Nevertheless, the peace accord had shown how a multiparty agreement between rival groups could be forged. And it added new impetus to moves to set up a negotiating forum.

Finding a starting point for negotiations had proved contentious enough. There were differing views on how a new constitution should be negotiated. The ANC insisted that the constitution should be drawn up by an elected assembly, so that each party's influence on the final document would be proportionate to its national support. The government wanted an unelected conference, comprising all political parties 'with a proven basis of support', to deliberate upon two critical issues: the composition, functioning and decision-making process of the actual constitutional negotiating conference, and the broad principles to be contained in a new constitution. It opposed the idea of a constituent assembly, fearing that it would allow a single party, or alliance of parties, emerging from an election with a commanding majority, virtually to write its own constitution – in effect predetermining constitutional issues which were supposed to be the subject of negotiation. The ANC demanded an interim government; the government said it had no intention of handing over power before the new constitution was in place. What was finally agreed was a multiparty conference, a date, an agenda and a venue.

It had taken nearly two years to get that far. It would take another two years before agreement on a new constitution was reached. There were times along the way when it seemed that the whole enterprise was doomed.

Chapter 4

From Breakdown to Breakthrough

The venue was a cavernous and gloomy complex normally used as a trade exhibition centre, close to Jan Smuts international airport on the outskirts of Johannesburg. On 20 December 1991, there assembled there the widest cross-section of political groups that had ever met in South Africa. The name given to the gathering was the Convention for a Democratic South Africa, popularly known as Codesa. The only similar gathering in South Africa had taken place more than 80 years earlier at the National Convention of 1908–9 designed to bring about a union between the British colonies of the Cape and Natal and the former Boer republics of the Transvaal and the Orange Free State which had been defeated in the Anglo-Boer war of 1899–1902. On that occasion no African representation was permitted. Now the aim was to achieve a wider settlement.

Invitations to Codesa had been sent to 23 parties. In all, 19 had accepted. These included the government and the National Party; the African National Congress, and its two allies, the South African Communist Party and the Transvaal and Natal Indian Congresses; the Inkatha Freedom Party; four 'independent' homeland governments; five 'self-governing' homeland parties; three parties from the Indian and Coloured parliaments; and the liberal parliamentary opposition party, the Democratic Party. Those who refused invitations included the radical Pan-Africanist Congress; the far-right Conservative Party; and the extremist Afrikaner Weerstandsbeweging (AWB). One other notable absentee was Buthelezi. Although Inkatha was present, Buthelezi had personally decided to stay away in protest against the turning down of his demand for two additional delegations, one headed by the king of the Zulus, Goodwill Zwelethini, the other representing the KwaZulu administration.

Codesa's first plenary session (Codesa 1) was largely a formality. Before handing over to a series of working groups, delegations were asked to sign a Declaration of Intent, consisting mainly of expressions of goodwill, which committed them to an undivided South Africa, a multiparty democracy with universal suffrage, a separation of powers, an independent judiciary and a bill of rights. Significantly, Inkatha chose to play a dissident role. It refused to sign the Declaration, arguing that the reference made to an 'undivided' South Africa implied that the federal system it wanted had been ruled out. Only when an amendment was later inserted, giving an assurance that the offending clause did not commit Codesa to a unitary state, did Inkatha sign.

What Codesa 1 was also memorable for was a dramatic confrontation between Mandela and de Klerk. Mandela had graciously conceded to de Klerk the right to the final speaking opportunity on the first day. De Klerk then used the occasion to lecture the ANC for its refusal to abandon the armed struggle, in the manner of a headmaster dealing with an errant child. Mandela responded with a ferocious personal attack on de Klerk. 'I am gravely concerned about the behaviour of Mr de Klerk today,' he began. He described de Klerk as 'the head of an illegitimate, discredited minority regime' who was 'not fit to be a head of government' and accused him of trickery and immorality. The spectacle on prime-time television of a white leader being abused by a black politician was an altogether new experience for South Africans. When it was all done, the two men shook hands. But it was not an auspicious beginning.

The working groups, where the horse-trading was to

take place before the next plenary session in May (Codesa 2), were assigned five areas of responsibility. Group One was to examine conditions needed to create a climate for free political participation; Group Two was given the task of deciding constitutional principles and a constitution-making process; Group Three was to deal with transitional arrangements for government in the period leading to a new constitution; Group Four was to consider the future of the 'independent' homelands – Transkei, Bophuthatswana, Ciskei and Venda; and Group Five was to look at time-frames and mechanisms for implementing the decisions of Codesa.

Exactly how decisions were to be taken was never clearly defined. It was agreed that no decision would be taken by Codesa unless there was 'sufficient consensus'. Sufficient consensus was described as consensus which would enable the process to proceed. In practice, this meant that if the government and the ANC agreed, then there was sufficient consensus; if they failed to agree, there was not. The only other parties at Codesa with enough stature to influence the decision-making process were the Democratic Party and Inkatha. But since Buthelezi remained aloof from the proceedings, Inkatha's role became of marginal importance; none of his delegates was willing to take an initiative without his approval.

What went on in the working groups was largely hidden from public view. The negotiators met behind closed doors. The only information available to the outside world therefore came in the form of leaks from participants who were hardly neutral. Many of the subjects under discussion, moreover, were of numbing complexity. The result consequently was a great deal of confusion outside Codesa about what was going on inside. Breakthrough and breakdown seemed to follow each other with increasing frequency.

At the core of the negotiations was the constitution-making process. In other words the question of how political power was to be apportioned. De Klerk entered the negotiations with the purpose not of transferring power, but of striking a unique power-sharing deal which would ensure a powerful role for the white minority in the future. His model of majority rule was not the standard version – 'simple majority rule', as he disparagingly referred to it – but a constitution which would entrench the position of minority parties in government and restrain majority parties through a maze of checks.

The proposals put forward by the National Party included: a transitional government of an enforced coalition for up to ten years, with a multiparty executive, a rotating presidency, and a strong emphasis on devolution of power to regional authorities; to this was added a bicameral parliament, the first house to be elected by proportional representation (which enhances the role of minorities), the second to be the seat of minorities, in which each party receiving a specified minimum support in elections would receive an equal number of seats; the second house would effectively have the power to veto legislation by the first house.

In de Klerk's view, the purpose of Codesa was to settle, in a multiparty forum, as many of these constitutional details as possible before the negotiating circus moved on to an elected assembly where the influence of minority parties was bound to be reduced. Only when the National Party's future was secure was he prepared to relinquish sole power. The transition, if necessary, would be a long one.

The ANC entered the negotiations with the aim of moving the process on rapidly from Codesa to an interim government and to an elected assembly empowered to determine a new constitution. The ANC wanted a radical rupture with the past. Codesa's role, in the ANC's view, was merely to decide what measures were needed before an assembly could be elected. It was anxious to achieve swift results. The slow progress so far made on the road to majority rule since 1990 had produced a groundswell of criticism from within its own ranks. Moreover, the

ANC's support in the townships was being undermined daily as a result of the level of violence there and the party's inability to provide protection.

While Codesa's working groups grappled with these issues, de Klerk's own support appeared to be dwindling. In a parliamentary by-election in the Orange Free State in November 1991, the National Party lost its seat to the Conservative Party in a spectacular swing against the government; in February 1992, the same happened in Potchefstroom. The government's faltering support was of more than ordinary significance. De Klerk had repeatedly promised that the white electorate would be allowed the final verdict on any agreement made about South Africa's future constitution. Rising white opposition to the government therefore placed the whole outcome of the negotiations in jeopardy. Rather than delay the matter any further, de Klerk, within days of the Potchefstroom defeat, announced the holding of a white referendum on the reform process. A clear majority in favour, he said, would obviate the need for the government to return to the white electorate. The risks he took were considerable. A defeat for the government would almost certainly have led to civil war. All the resources of the white establishment were thrown into securing a 'Yes' vote. The ANC did its best to reassure whites about the future of the negotiating process, promising job security to civil servants and urging a 'Yes' vote.

The result was a triumph for de Klerk. About 85 per cent of the white electorate of 3.3 million turned out to vote; 68 per cent said 'Yes'. Only one out of 15 regions recorded a majority 'No' vote – Pietersburg, in the strongly conservative northern Transvaal. Even Pretoria, which for so long symbolised Afrikanerdom in all its might, produced a 57 per cent 'Yes' vote. 'It doesn't often happen that in one generation a nation gets the opportunity to rise above itself,' declared de Klerk. 'The white electorate has risen above itself in this referendum.'

In the euphoria which followed the referendum, it

seemed that few other obstacles remained in the way of a settlement. Indeed, Codesa was noted for its convivial and cosy atmosphere, where participants, wining and dining lavishly at the state's expense, were afforded every opportunity to come to terms after the tedious business of the working groups.

In many areas under negotiation, considerable progress was in fact made. The reality, however, was that the two main participants – the government and the ANC – had come no closer to agreement on what the real role of Codesa should be, let alone the details of a new constitution. As the deadline for Codesa 2 approached, the negotiators in Working Group Two were seen to be engaged in a haggle over percentages needed to adopt certain constitutional clauses: the ANC wanted 70 per cent; the government insisted on 75 per cent. To the outside world, it seemed that all that stood in the way of a historic agreement was a matter of five per cent. But though important in itself, this particular dispute obscured the more fundamental divisions in the position of the government and the ANC. The government was prepared to haggle indefinitely. Indeed, it believed that the slower the transition proceeded, the better. Its confidence was bolstered in particular by the results of the referendum; de Klerk had finally dispensed with the right-wing threat he feared so much. The ANC, however, was alarmed not only by the lack of any real progress being made at Codesa but by signs that it had begun to lose touch with its constituency as the negotiations dragged on. Radicals within the ANC were highly critical of its handling of the negotiations and wanted a more aggressive approach. When Codesa 2 reached deadlock on May 16, amid acrimonious exchanges, the ANC was already preparing alternative plans.

The strategy the ANC adopted carried high risks. It involved a campaign of mass action, a series of rolling strikes, demonstrations and boycotts across the country, organised with the help of the ANC's allies, the trade union federation, Cosatu, and the South African Communist Party, and intended to force the government to back down at the negotiating table. The climax was to be a general strike. Most groups within the 'tripartite alliance' regarded mass action as a necessary component of the negotiating process. A radical faction, however, saw it not as a means of gaining compromises, but as a way of bringing the government down. The radicals pointed to events in Eastern Europe, especially to Leipzig, where street demonstrations had caused governments to fall, and believed that the same could be engineered in South Africa. Among those favouring the 'Leipzig option' was Ronnie Kasrils, a leading communist and senior Umkhonto official, with romantic notions of what revolutionary action could achieve and clearly bored by the proceedings at Codesa which he rarely attended. Kasrils was given charge of mass action activity.

Yet mass action was to be launched at a time when many townships were already in turmoil. The National Peace Accord, signed with such flourish in 1991, had proved fruitless; many of its committees were close to collapse. The death toll, since its introduction, had reached 1,500. The Reef War continued unabated. Between July 1990, when it started, and April 1992, at least 260 attacks on township residents by hostel dwellers had been recorded. All previous experience of strikes, boycotts and demonstrations showed that they led to an upsurge in violence as supporters resorted to coercion to get their way. The risk now was that the turmoil and violence might become uncontrollable.

The date chosen for the start of the mass action campaign was June 16, the anniversary of the beginning of the Soweto revolt in 1976. The ANC proclaimed the mass stayaway it organised a success; the government said the stayaway would have happened on that date anyway. There then occurred an incident of such brutality that, just like Sharpeville and Soweto, its name came to be remembered around the world and to be a landmark in the passage of South Africa's violent history. It plunged the country into a crisis far worse than anyone had expected.

On the night of June 17, a group of hostel dwellers in Boipatong, a small township in the Vaal Triangle, 40 miles south of Johannesburg, attacked a nearby shack settlement, kicking in doors, smashing windows and then hacking, stabbing and shooting residents at random in a killing spree lasting more than four hours, leaving 45 residents dead, mostly women and children. It was the fourth mass killing that week in a black area near Johannesburg. The police were once again accused of collusion. Two days later three people died when police opened fire on a crowd which had gathered to protest at the massacre.

Mandela suspended all talks with the government. 'I can no longer explain to our people why we continue to talk to a regime that is murdering our people and conducting war against us.' The negotiation process, he said, was 'completely in tatters'. Indeed, all that was left of it in public, it seemed, was an angry exchange of memoranda. When de Klerk paid a visit to Boipatong to show his sympathy, he was insulted and chased away by angry youths within minutes. At the funeral of the victims, speaker after speaker called for the intensification of mass action and his overthrow. 'Mandela, we want arms now,' read the placards.

De Klerk's difficulties were compounded by the continuing trickle of evidence implicating security forces in violent activity. In April 1992, a white police captain and four black 'special constables' were convicted of the killing of eleven people – six women, three men and two children – in a small rural town in Natal, whom they believed were supporters of the ANC. The 'special constables' were Inkatha men who had been selected and trained by the police. The judge's verdict was that the massacre was part of a security force operation to disrupt the community, oust an established ANC-aligned resident's association and give Inkatha control of the area. In his evidence, the police captain, Brian Mitchell, said he saw himself as a soldier in a civil war in which the enemy were pro-ANC groups. The murders had been carried out in 1988, but Mitchell's views were still common among white police officers. Within days of Mitchell's conviction, it was revealed that a former member of the KwaZulu police force serving a 27-year sentence for murder, whom a judge had described as a 'beast in policeman's clothing', had been released from prison in February 1992 after serving less than one year of his sentence. 'The rot goes deep,' commented a Johannesburg newspaper.

The military too were implicated. In May 1992, the press published the contents of a military intelligence signal proposing the 'permanent removal' of four prominent black activists in the Eastern Cape, including Matthew Goniwe. Three weeks after the signal was sent, the killings took place. The incident had occurred in 1985. But the disclosure seven years later of military involvement not only stirred black anger against the army but reinforced all the fears and suspicions harboured about the activities of a 'third force'. The man who authorised the signal was Brigadier Christoffel Van Der Westhuizen, then Head of Joint Operations at the Eastern Cape Province command. In 1992, General Van Der Westhuizen was Chief of Military Intelligence.

It was the Department of Military Intelligence (DMI) which was the main focus of suspicions. For years, the DMI had been in control of special force operations supporting Renamo rebels in Mozambique and Unita rebels in Angola fighting to overthrow their respective Marxist governments. It had also been involved in training Inkatha members. The units which the DMI had run across South Africa's borders – like 32 Battalion, composed mainly of Portuguese-speaking mercenaries – had returned to South Africa once the DMI's campaign of destabilisation in neighbouring countries had come to an end and once the war in Namibia was over. Many senior officers were bitterly resentful of the outcome.

In a pre-referendum message to soldiers who fought in Angola and Namibia, Colonel Jan Breytenbach, a former commander of the much-feared 32 Battalion, reflected their discontent. 'You did not lose in Angola,' he told them. 'You did not lose in Namibia. You were betrayed by politicians under foreign pressure.' From their bases in South Africa, these special force units provided a ready source of recruits for disgruntled officers intent on organising covert operations. Other irregular units included Koevoet, a police counter-insurgency force once used in Namibia, many of whose members were now active in the South African police force. All had been trained to hunt down ANC or Swapo cadres in the streets and shebeens of southern Africa and were prone to violent and lawless conduct.

Evidence of how far the DMI was prepared to go in pursuing its enemies surfaced in July, on the eve of a United Nations Security Council debate on South Africa, much to de Klerk's embarrassment. A London newspaper reported that two DMI officers had entered Britain in April on a mission to plan the assassination of the police defector, Dirk Coetzee, with the help of Irish paramilitaries. The two officers had been arrested and then deported to South Africa. One of them was a former secretary to General Van Der Westhuizen. 'The suspicion remains,' said the Johannesburg *Star*, 'that de Klerk is not master in his own house, that his security forces, or elements among them, do not share his reformist goals.'

Given the task of sorting out the evidence, the judicial commission into violence headed by Judge Richard Goldstone came to the conclusion, after six months of hearings around the country, that the primary cause of the violence was not security force activity but the political battle between supporters of the ANC and Inkatha. 'Both sides resort to violence and intimidation in their attempts to gain control over geographic areas,' it said. The commission exonerated de Klerk himself and his government from any direct involvement in political violence. It had received no evidence justifying allegations of 'any direct complicity in or planning of current violence'. But it sharply rebuked the government for failing to implement earlier recommendations it had made, including the need to impose security measures at hostels and to ban the carrying of all dangerous weapons. The commission also noted that its previous recommendation regarding the withdrawal from townships of 32 Battalion (whose members had been found responsible for rape and other assaults during 'peace-keeping' operations) had been blocked by the army commander, General George Meiring. The government, said the commission, 'must be able to demonstrate that it has control over its security forces'.

Police actions were also severely criticised. An independent inquiry into the Boipatong massacre, carried out by a British criminologist and two senior British officers, concluded in July 1992 that while there was no evidence of police or government complicity, the police were to blame for 'a failure of leadership at all levels'; it described as incompetent the force's general systems and organisational structure.

Pressing on with mass action, the ANC alliance brought the campaign to a climax in early August with a general strike by several million workers. Much of the country's business and industry came to a halt or was forced to reduce output. The strike was followed by mass marches. In Pretoria, Mandela led more than 50,000 supporters through the heart of the city to the seat of white government, Union Buildings. 'Today we are at the door of Union Buildings,' declared Cyril Ramaphosa, one of Mandela's key aides. 'Next time, F. W. de Klerk, we are going to be inside your office.' Mandela himself proclaimed the strike as 'unquestionably one of the great events in our history'.

Yet for all the fervour that mass action achieved, it produced nothing in terms of moving the government from its entrenched position. Nor was it a strategy that ANC supporters could afford to continue indefinitely. The ANC was divided over what to do next. Some wanted to seek a way back into negotiations. Radical activists, however, argued that though mass action would not bring Pretoria to its knees, it would work against weaker governments in the homelands, in KwaZulu, Bophuthatswana and Ciskei, the allies of Pretoria which had so far kept a tight clamp on all ANC activity.

Ciskei was a particularly tempting target. Here was the soft underbelly of the homelands system. It was ruled by a military dictator, Brigadier Oupa Gqozo, who had only recently seized power and who had increasingly resorted to repressive measures to stay there. Its capital, Bisho, was close to the 'border' with South Africa and adjacent to an area where the ANC's following was strong. A mass march on Bisho, so the radical activists calculated, could trigger a switch of allegiance by Ciskei soldiers and public servants, causing the homeland administration to collapse.

On the morning of September 7, a column of 70,000 marchers set out from King William's Town along the road to Bisho. Their aim, according to one leading activist, was 'to drive the pig from the barn'. The border was closed by a line of razor wire, with Ciskei troops deployed behind it. Scouting ahead of the column, Ronnie Kasrils, one of the main organisers, noticed a gap in the outer fence of a stadium alongside the road, which seemed to offer a route into the centre of Bisho. Returning back down the hill to colleagues, Kasrils urged that he should lead a breakaway group from the main column, storm through the gap and head on to Bisho. But he had failed to spot a detachment of troops covering the gap from trench positions. As Kasril's group raced through the gap, the troops opened fire, killing 28 marchers. Bisho had joined Sharpeville, Soweto and Boipatong as a byword for bloodshed and brutality.

The mood in South Africa in late 1992 came ever closer to despair. On all fronts the country seemed to be in the grip of ill-fortune. The endless cycles of violence were but one aspect. A catastrophic drought had laid waste to farming areas. The economy was sunk in the third year of recession with no end to it in sight. The very institutions of government, it seemed, were rotten: the police proven incompetent; the military contaminated by dirty tricks. Corruption was everywhere in the air: white civil servants and politicians scrambled to top up their pension funds and fix long-term contracts before the day of reckoning. Security officials insisted on indemnities. The columnist, Shaun Johnson, wrote in the *Star*: 'If you stand on a street corner in Pretoria late at night, I am sure you can hear the sound of shredders shredding. Of assets being stripped. Of pockets being stuffed.' One by one, new scandals emerged. Official investigations into the Lebowa homeland unearthed incompetence and corruption on a vast scale: entire departments had been created without government authorisation; non-existent officials had been paid for years; huge funds intended for buying school books and stationery had disappeared without trace. In KwaNdebele, white security officials, in connivance with homeland politicians, were shown to be involved in a wide range of excesses including the murder and detention without trial of children as young as eleven years old. At the Department of Development Aid, funds worth billions of rands earmarked for underdeveloped rural areas had been siphoned off into private bank accounts. Investigations by the Goldstone Commission uncovered a secret operation set up in 1991 by the Department of Military Intelligence involving a double murderer who had been hired to lead a covert unit that would use prostitutes, homosexuals and drug-dealers in a dirty tricks attempt to discredit the ANC's armed wing, Umkhonto. On top of all this was the crippling stalemate within the political arena. After three years of effort, the politicians, entrenched in positions of stubbornness and defiance, had little to show and, what was worse, nothing to offer. Whatever confidence there was about the country's future was rapidly ebbing away, both at home and abroad.

So deep was the crisis that it induced on both sides a willingness to compromise that had not existed before. In the wake of Bisho, Mandela called a halt to mass action, reprimanding Kasrils for his recklessness; no further adventures in the homelands would be countenanced. The priority was to pull South Africa 'out of the quagmire'. De Klerk responded with the offer of a summit meeting. On September 26, less than three weeks after the Bisho shooting, they signed a Record of Understanding. De Klerk agreed to a number of specific concessions, including the release of 500 ANC prisoners, new security measures at migrant worker hostels and a ban on the carrying of dangerous weapons. But the real significance of the summit was that it marked the point at which political bargaining shifted from multiparty talks to bilateral talks.

Reform of the security forces was pushed through. In an attempt to restore the credibility of the police, 13 generals were retired, nearly one quarter of the general staff; an independent civilian body was set up with powers to review police actions; officers were sent for retraining in community policing; and affirmative action was approved to promote non-whites to top ranks. De Klerk also moved to clean up the military, sacking or suspending 23 officers including two generals and ordering a purge of military intelligence staff Special Force units like 32 Battalion and the police counter-insurgency unit, Koevoet, were disbanded. Military personnel and their associates, said de Klerk, 'have been involved, and in some cases are still involved, in illegal and unauthorised activities and malpractices. There are indications that some of the activities and some of the individuals might have been motivated by a wish to prevent us from succeeding in our goals'.

On the negotiations front, there were also signs of compromise. In an article in the Communist Party journal *African Communist*, the Party Chairman, Joe Slovo, a central figure on the ANC's radical wing, suggested that in order to break the deadlock it might be necessary for the ANC to offer the government 'a sunset clause' in a new constitution which would entrench power-sharing for a fixed period, as an alternative to making a bid for total power. The ANC might also have to give ground by offering guarantees on regional government and an amnesty for security officers, and by honouring the contracts of civil servants, either by retaining them or compensating them. 'The ANC is not dealing with a defeated enemy; an early revolutionary seizure of power is not realistic; the capacity of the white civil service, army and police to destabilise a newly born democracy is enormous; and a sunset clause should be inserted in the new constitution to provide for compulsory power-sharing for a fixed number of years.' To emphasise the point, Slovo warned: 'All we will achieve when we have won the election is to gain political office. We would not gain state power in the sense of having a complete transformation on day one of the police, the armed forces, the judiciary and the civil services.' Coming from a figure so highly respected by ANC radicals, these ideas carried all the more weight.

The ANC developed these suggestions in a document entitled *Negotiations: A Strategic Perspective* which was formally adopted in November. Because of the pressure on the ANC to achieve results and the government's ability to 'endlessly delay', it said, there was a need to make compromises and to pursue a swift negotiation process. This process would have to address questions of job security, retrenchment packages and a general amnesty for 'all armed formations and sections of the civil service'. Of crucial importance, the ANC argued in favour of a government of national unity. 'We also need to accept ... that, even after the adoption of a new constitution, the balance of forces and the interests of the country ... may still require us to consider ... a government of national unity.' The way forward, it suggested, was for the government and the ANC to reach bilateral agreement on these issues before including other parties in a multiparty forum.

There were the makings of a deal here. De Klerk added

to the momentum by committing himself to a clear time frame for the transfer of power, suggesting 1994 as the pivotal year. In bilateral discussions, government and ANC delegates soon reached common ground on the outline for a new order. This involved a transitional executive council preparing the way for elections to a constituent assembly and an interim government which would comprise all parties winning an agreed share of the vote. The interim government would rule South Africa for five years or more while a final constitution was drawn up and would allow a strong role for regional government, providing enhanced security for minority and regional interests. The final constitution, drawn up by the constituent assembly, would be based on a set of principles agreed to previously at the multiparty negotiations which would launch the whole process.

The growing rapprochement between de Klerk and the ANC provoked a fit of rage from Buthelezi who resented being left on the sidelines. He denounced de Klerk's 'appeasement' of the ANC and poured scorn on the ANC's threat to march on his capital, Ulundi, reminding it of the grim fate of a British army column which had invaded Zululand in 1879. Zulus, he said, were ready for another 'washing of the spears'. Buthelezi now played the tribal card for all it was worth, presenting himself as the defender of all Zulus against external enemies like the ANC and its communist allies bent on their destruction. At mass rallies, he warned Zulus that their very existence was at stake, that their foes planned to wipe KwaZulu 'off the face of the earth'. Claiming that secret deals were being made, he withdrew from negotiations with the government.

De Klerk's dilemma was considerable. An agreement with the ANC formed the whole basis of his plan for a settlement: not only did the ANC have massive internal support but it held the key to international recognition and the lifting of sanctions. An agreement with Inkatha was not so essential, but it formed a major part of de

Klerk's hopes of forging an electoral alliance of regional black leaders, of whom Buthelezi was the most important. Buthelezi's national support was of little consequence but his following in KwaZulu/Natal, according to opinion polls, was still substantial. His pro-capitalist policies were far more compatible with National Party ideology than the ANC's plans for 'redistribution'. Moreover, a significant section of the National Party, the military and the police, as well as a bevy of white businessmen in Natal, much preferred Buthelezi as an ally to the prospect of having to do business with the likes of Mandela. For de Klerk, however, Buthelezi's volatile behaviour and his penchant for obstruction made him an unreliable ally.

In December, the day before the government and the ANC were due to hold a *bosberaad*, a bush summit, Buthelezi suddenly unveiled proposals of his own for an autonomous region for KwaZulu/Natal, threatening a 'go-it-alone' approach if a referendum in the territory approved the plan, all of which de Klerk was obliged publicly to repudiate. Even more bizarre was Buthelezi's decision to throw in his lot with a group of other homeland leaders and conservative white politicians, none of whom had credentials as good as his own. They included the military dictator of Ciskei, Brigadier Oupa Gqozo, the autocratic ruler of Bophuthatswana, Lucas Mangope, and the leaderships of the far-right Conservative Party and the breakaway Afrikaner Volksunie whose sole purpose was to obtain an Afrikaner homeland. Together they launched the Concerned South African Group, otherwise known as Cosag, disclaiming at first any intention of forming an alliance, but drawing ever closer and eventually operating as one. The link between them was that they all favoured the idea of self-determination and wanted the new South Africa to be a federation of powerful regions. But it was an alliance that was to cost Buthelezi much credibility and support.

The ANC had its own difficulties in trying to sell a compromise deal on power-sharing to its radical faction.

In an extraordinary attack on the ANC leadership, Winnie Mandela claimed that the negotiating process was being conducted between 'the élite of the oppressed and the oppressors', ignoring the interests of the masses. 'The NP élite is getting into bed with the ANC in order to preserve its silken sheets. And the leadership of the ANC is getting into bed with the NP to enjoy this new-found luxury. The concern is that this new amalgam of power is promoting its own self-interest and overlooking the plight and needs of the under-privileged masses . . . The quick-fix solutions sought by our leaders can only benefit a few and will backfire massively on the country as a whole.' A new breed of leadership was needed, she said, truly representative of the aspirations of the 'oppressed'.

Winnie Mandela's reputation at the time had sunk to a low ebb. Her criminal record as the convicted kidnapper of a 14-year-old boy who was subsequently brutally beaten and then murdered by a member of her bodyguard known as the Mandela Football Club provided a major source of embarrassment for Mandela and for the ANC. The judge at her trial had described her as 'a calm, composed, deliberate and unblushing liar'. Other public disclosures about her affair with a young ANC lawyer, which persisted for two years after Mandela's release from prison, and the luxury trips they had made together to the United States, added to a growing sense of revulsion in some ANC quarters about her conduct. There were also allegations about her misuse of party funds. In mid-1992, Winnie Mandela was forced to resign all her official positions, as head of the ANC's welfare department, as chair of the ANC's Women's League and as a member of the ANC's National Executive Committee. Her husband, Nelson, who had felt obliged to stand by her out of a sense of guilt at the lack of support he had been able to give from prison while the South African authorities harassed and persecuted her year after year, was finally persuaded of the need to announce a separation. But Winnie's lust for power was not so easily thwarted. Determined to rebuild her political career, she cultivated popularity in the squatter camps in the Johannesburg area, handing out food and blankets, and amongst militant youths, appearing at rallies in combat fatigues and launching abusive attacks on the police and the government. The populist rhetoric she used in denouncing ANC leaders for selling out the 'oppressed' found a ready audience; and the impact she made was hard to ignore.

Another contender for power, the Pan-Africanist Congress, also made its presence felt. The PAC had played only a marginal role since its unbanning in 1990. Its rhetoric was still tied firmly to the idea of armed struggle – 'one settler–one bullet' was a favourite slogan – though neither in the 1970s and the 1980s when Umkhonto was active nor since had this amounted to anything more than the murder of a few policemen. Its demand for 'African' control of South Africa and the 'return of the land' was a potentially powerful message, but its leadership was inept. The PAC had refused to participate in Codesa, arguing that it was merely a device to protect white privilege. But as a new round of negotiations approached, it clearly felt the need to raise its profile. Towards the end of 1992, its armed wing, the Azanian People's Liberation Army (Apla), carried out attacks on white civilians on farms in the Orange Free State, on a restaurant in Queenstown, and at a country club in King William's Town where a Christmas celebration was underway, adding yet more to the death toll. Having thus advertised itself and achieved universal condemnation, the PAC let it be known that it was willing to hold talks with the government on ways to end violence in the country.

In April 1993, after months of haggling, a new gathering of political groups, even more representative of the political spectrum than the cross-section at Codesa fifteen months before, assembled at the World Trade Centre. This time, the Conservative Party was present, forsaking its vow never to sit down with 'terrorists'. So was its offshoot, the Afrikaner Volksunie. Places had also been found for traditional leaders, like the Zulu monarch, King Goodwill Zwelethini, whose presence had been repeatedly demanded previously by Buthelezi. Also around the table was the Pan-Africanist Congress, still mixing dialogue with terrorism. In all, 26 groups attended. No agreement on what the new negotiating forum should be called was ever reached, so it was given no formal name.

Within days, however, before any progress was possible, South Africa was thrust to the brink of a catastrophe far greater than any that had occurred before. On April 10, a white gunman shot dead Chris Hani, a prominent ANC leader, in the driveway of his home in a predominantly white suburb in the gold-mining town of Boksburg, east of Johannesburg. Hani was a hero to millions of black youths, a legendary guerrilla commander who had risen to become Umkhonto's chief of staff and a lifelong communist who championed the cause of the poor and dispossessed. He was tough, ruthless and hugely popular, second only to Mandela according to an independent poll in November 1992. He was also famous for fiery speech-making and was unusual among the ANC's young leaders in that he could strike a chord as much with agricultural workers as with township residents. But it was his following, his influence, among the youth that was unique. When Hani spoke, they listened. If anyone was capable of mobilising this vast unruly constituency behind the negotiation process, it was Hani. Since his return to South Africa in 1990, he had been converted to the cause of negotiation, though not without misgivings. When radical activists advocated a break with negotiations, Hani had argued determinedly in favour of pursuing them. He was pragmatic about the need to offer security forces an amnesty, and disparaging about the PAC's efforts to continue its armed attacks. When self-defence units in the townships began degenerating into vigilante gangs, he had been the first to call for their disbanding. A few days before his death, he had declared: 'I am now a combatant for peace.'

To the far right of white politics, however, Hani was

the epitome of a communist terrorist, a demon figure constantly the target of right-wing newspapers. A few days before the assassin struck, a government minister had described Umkhonto as 'a bunch of animals'; and an influential newspaper had told its readers that Hani was assembling a vengeful 'Black People's Army'. In a recent interview, he had said: 'The message is being sent to the white population that Chris Hani is the devil himself.' Many whites believed consequently that Hani 'had it coming to him'.

So great was the anger within the black community that it threatened to ignite violence on a scale never seen before in South Africa. With remarkable speed, the leadership of the crisis was assumed not by the government but by the ANC and Mandela. On radio and television throughout the day, ANC officials appealed for peace. Mandela, who was on holiday in Transkei, rushed back to Johannesburg to make a national address on television. 'With all the authority at my command, I appeal to all our people to remain calm and to honour the memory of Chris Hani by remaining a disciplined force for peace.'

Seeking to harness the tide of outrage, the ANC announced a week-long campaign of mass protest, including a national stayaway and memorial services. The risks of violence breaking out from such action were only too well known. On the eve of a day of mourning declared by the ANC, Mandela again made an address to the nation on radio and television. 'Tonight', he began, 'I am reaching out to every single South African, black and white, from the very depths of my being.' The assassin, he said, was a white man. But it was a white woman of Afrikaner origin, a witness to the murder, who had helped to bring him to justice. He appealed for calm, discipline and dignified conduct. 'Chris Hani was a soldier. He believed in iron discipline ... Any lack of discipline is trampling on the values that Chris Hani stood for. Those who commit such acts serve only the interests of the assassins.'

By the standards to which South Africa had become

accustomed, the events in the days following Hani's assassination passed relatively peacefully. Several million participated in memorial services. In nearly every urban area chanting crowds swept through city centres; in several they left streets in chaos, with burnt cars, smashed and looted shops. But mostly the demonstrators heeded Mandela's call for discipline. In Johannesburg, the ANC reached a formal agreement with the authorities for the joint policing of memorial marches through the city, to reduce the danger of violence. Some four million workers responded to the stayaway call, again in relative calm. But the sheer size and intensity of feeling of the protests was something white authority had never before experienced. There was no mistaking the clamour for revenge among radical activists. The ANC's youth leader, Peter Mokaba, was shown on television chanting, 'Kill the boers, Kill the farmers', a refrain also taken up by Winnie Mandela. At a memorial service in Soweto when Nelson Mandela referred to a message of sympathy from the National Party, he was jeered. The PAC claimed that Hani's killing justified their own armed attacks. Nor was there any mistaking the growing impatience at the failure of the negotiation process to deliver concrete results. 'Mandela released three years ago: South Africa still not free,' read one placard at Hani's funeral.

The significance of these events, however, went far beyond the question of violence. It was the time when Mandela emerged as a national leader, comprehending the magnitude of the crisis, seeking to calm white fears as well as black anger, demanding discipline and receiving it. De Klerk and the government, meanwhile, were hardly to be seen. De Klerk issued statements, clearly partisan in nature, aimed at white constituents alarmed by the violence which followed the assassination. He showed little understanding of the anger and loss felt by the black majority. His preoccupation, as one Johannesburg newspaper noted, was 'to assure whites that they were safe from the black hordes'. As the courts were later to prove, the assassination of Chris Hani was the work of a Polish immigrant, resident in South Africa for twelve years, and a Conservative Party MP, Clive Derby-Lewis, an inane act carried out in the name of white supremacy and anti-communism. The irony was that, in the long struggle between de Klerk and Mandela for possession of South Africa, no other single event provoked such a dramatic shift in the balance of power, nor revealed so clearly to the white community how important Mandela was to their future security.

Mandela's demands for swift, tangible progress in the negotiations now became irresistible. In May, at the multiparty negotiations at the World Trade Centre, 23 of the 26 parties represented there signed a Declaration of Intent agreeing that elections for a new government would be held no later than April 1994. The Conservative Party refused to sign.

As the spectre of majority rule moved closer, the white far right made determined efforts to present a united front in its demands for an Afrikaner homeland. Under the tutelage of a 'Committee of Generals' consisting of retired army and police commanders from the 'total strategy' era, led by a former chief of the South African Defence Force, General Constand Viljoen, the Afrikaner Volksfront (AVF) was launched in May, bringing together 21 organisations including the Conservative Party, the neo-Nazi Afrikaner Weerstandsbeweging (AWB), the Transvaal Municipal Associations, white trade unions and farmers' unions from the Transvaal and the Orange Free State. Viljoen, with a distinguished military career behind him, had hoped to establish a respectable image for the AVF, but he was unable to contend with the antics of the AWB.

At a demonstration organised by the AVF outside the World Trade Centre to back its demands for an Afrikaner homeland, a group of AWB supporters, brandishing shotguns and revolvers, broke through a police cordon, drove an armoured security vehicle through the glass frontage of the building and stormed into the conference chamber, assaulting delegates, officials and journalists along the way. They then occupied delegates' seats, scrawled slogans on walls and urinated on the floor. Viljoen was left to apologise for this 'poor conduct'.

The negotiators ploughed on doggedly. In July, the first draft of an interim constitution emerged. It provided for a bicameral parliament consisting of a 400-member National Assembly elected by proportional representation from national and regional party lists and a Senate elected indirectly by regional legislatures, and a cabinet representative of parties occupying a specified percentage of seats. The National Assembly and the Senate would form a constitution-making body to draw up a final constitution based on a set of previously agreed principles. To accommodate demands for a federal dispensation, the first draft included provisions for establishing regional legislatures with a wide range of power over regional activity. Elections to regional legislatures would take place at the same time as national elections. The regional bodies would then draw up their own constitutions which would have to be consistent with constitutional principles previously agreed and in line with the final national constitution. In the run-up to the national elections – set for 27 April 1994 – a Transitional Executive Council would be given powers to ensure that the 'playing field' was level.

The Conservative Party described the document as 'hostile to Afrikaner interests' and a 'recipe for civil war, further economic deterioration and a spiral of violence'. Its new leader, Ferdi Hartzenberg, said the Conservative Party would participate in further talks only when Afrikaner self-determination was 'unequivocally accepted'.

Buthelezi's reaction was equally hostile. He demanded greater powers for the regions, in line with his own constitutional proposals for KwaZulu/Natal; he objected to the two-stage approach to the drafting of the final constitution, insisting that the full text should be drawn up by the present negotiators before an election rather than by an elected constitution-making body in the future; and in protest against the setting of the April date for the elections, he walked out of the negotations, clearly expecting them to founder in the same way as they had done the previous year when the ANC withdrew from Codesa 2. His language became increasingly strident and bellicose.

A second draft interim constitution in August conceded greater powers to regional government. But still Buthelezi rejected it. Together with his colleagues in Cosag – Mangope from Bophuthatswana, Gqozo from Ciskei, Hartzenberg from the Conservative Party – and joined by General Viljoen from the AVF, Buthelezi formed a 'Freedom Alliance' determined to press for a federal or confederal state and, with a warning of civil war 'or worse', he threatened to boycott the April elections unless his demands were met.

Parts of South Africa, in fact, already resembled a battlefield. While negotiators at the World Trade Centre had been picking their way through constitutional niceties, the orgy of violence elsewhere in the country had reached new peaks. In Cape Town, at a Sunday evening church meeting, gunmen burst in hurling hand grenades and spraying bullets into the mainly white congregation, killing eleven and injuring 50 people; Apla was suspected of carrying out the attack. In a dawn raid on a house in Transkei, said to be an Apla base, army commandos killed two children aged twelve, two aged 16 and a 19-year-old youth. On the Witwatersrand, the Reef War burst out anew. Townships on the East Rand like Thokosa and Katlehong were like war zones, their streets lined with deserted, burnt-out houses, wrecked vehicles, barricades and boulders, as Inkatha hostel dwellers and ANC comrades fought for territorial possession. Many hostel dwellers found themselves virtually under armed siege. Public transport came to a complete standstill; taxis refused to enter areas near hostels; train services were discontinued after train drivers were threatened, food and other supplies had to be delivered under paramilitary police protection. Hostels were packed not only with migrant workers but with whole families seeking protection from comrades in the townships; some had become virtually independent communities with their own schools, churches and *spaza* shops. Outside, in the townships, hit-and-run raids continued relentlessly. Close to a hostel in Germiston, gunmen with AK47s flagged down a minibus-taxi, ordered all the passengers out, selected Zulu-speaking passengers and executed them. In apparent retaliation, a three-man gang opened fire on a burial society meeting in the same location; all the victims were Xhosa-speaking. Nineteen people were massacred at a taxi queue in Johannesburg. Radical activists fanned the flames of violence for their own ends. At a mass funeral in Tembisa for the victims of a raid launched by members of a criminal gang called the Toasters, which used a local hostel as their base, the ANC's youth leader, Peter Mokaba, called on the funeral crowd 'to help me demolish that hostel ... brick by brick' and told them to drive the police and the army out of the townships and 'take the war to white areas'. 'Save your bullets ... Direct your guns at de Klerk.' The police were already constant targets of attack. 'Sometimes people kill policemen just for the fun of it,' a police spokesman commented. Paramilitary police units, unpopular and feared for their heavy-handed tactics, were in danger of ceding 'no-go' areas. As communities disintegrated, former ANC self-defence units, which had degenerated into vigilante gangs, running extortion rackets and setting up kangaroo courts, began their own territorial wars. 'These people will kill for anybody and can be used to settle any score,' an independent peace monitor reported. In the first ten months of 1993, some 1,300 people died in political violence in the East Rand townships. Similar strife occurred in the killing fields of KwaZulu/Natal, though on an even greater scale.

Back at the World Trade Centre, negotiators, exhausted

after seven months of haggling, drafting and redrafting, deadlocks and deadlines, nudged on by anxious businessmen and foreign diplomats, struggled through to the last remaining points of dispute. Hours before the final plenary session was due to sit on November 17, several crucial issues were still outstanding. In a frenetic burst of horse-trading, the government and the ANC emerged with what was termed a 'six-pack' deal. The government backed down on its insistence that cabinet decisions be taken by a two-thirds majority, agreeing instead that they should be made within 'the consensus-seeking spirit' of the negotiations. The ANC dropped its insistence on new elections as soon as a new constitution was in place, agreeing that national elections would not be held until 1999, thus giving the government of national unity elected in 1994 a five-year life span. Of crucial significance, the government gave way to the ANC's demand for a single ballot paper for the election of national and provincial legislatures rather than separate ballot papers for each, thus weakening the prospects of smaller regionally-based parties in the election. The smaller parties railed against the procedure, but to no avail.

Just after midnight on November 18, the interim constitution was approved by the plenary session. Mandela declared: 'Whereas apartheid deprived millions of our people of their citizenship, we are restoring that citizenship. Whereas apartheid sought to fragment our country, we are reuniting our country.' He urged South Africans to 'join hands and march into the future'. De Klerk was similarly effusive: 'We are on the threshold of a new era,' he said. 'South Africa will never be the same again.'

But there was still some way to go.

Chapter 5

Interregnum

In the euphoria which enveloped negotiators at the end of such a marathon endeavour, the pitfalls of a political settlement which did not include all players tended to be overlooked. The scent of power was a particularly heady experience for the ANC. 'A famous victory,' wrote Joe Slovo, the ANC's key strategist in the journal, *African Communist*. 'We got pretty much what we wanted.' The ANC's chief negotiator, Cyril Ramaphosa, crowed about how the National Party's negotiating position at the last hour had 'collapsed'. Despite widespread protests at the exclusion of a double ballot paper for use in the election, the ANC refused to compromise; the issue, it said, was not negotiable. When, in December, members of the Freedom Alliance presented a list of demands which included greater regional autonomy and a constitutional principle on the right of self-determination, as their terms for participating in the election, de Klerk was sympathetic, but ANC negotiators showed no patience with them. At early meetings of the Transitional Executive Council, the ANC was quick to throw its weight around with proposals for South African police intervention in KwaZulu and the freezing of a loan to Bophuthatswana. Given any sign of trouble from the provinces, a senior ANC official warned, they would 'let the tanks roll in'. In dealing with issues like the name of Kwazulu, the response was similarly curt: the name KwaZulu was a creation of apartheid and would not feature on maps of post-apartheid South Africa, declared Ramaphosa; henceforth KwaZulu/Natal would be known simply as Natal.

Whatever prospects there were of broadening the settlement to include Inkatha and other members of the Freedom Alliance rapidly degenerated. In intermittent negotiations, positions hardened. At a special Inkatha congress held at Ulundi at the end of January, an American evangelist set the tone, proclaiming loudly: 'Blessed is the spoiler, for he is spoiling the work of the devil.' The devil's agents, in Inkatha's view, now included not only the ANC and the Communist Party, but the National Party government and de Klerk. Buthelezi rejected Inkatha's participation in the election and spoke of the politics of resistance. 'It is impossible for me to lie to you and reassure you that the IFP's opposition to fighting the election under the present constitution will not bring casualties and even death,' he said. 'But we must resist the ANC and their communist surrogates. We are the only thing that stands in the way of their quest for power.' He urged followers to 'fight back', telling them: 'This is a region where we dominate. No foreign forces shall come into it to rule over us.' Buthelezi was venturing from the arena of political conflict into the murky realms of ethnic mobilisation.

His ultimate weapon was the Zulu king, Goodwill Zwelethini. Relations between the two men – Buthelezi was the king's uncle – had not always been easy. As both manoeuvred for influence after the establishment of the KwaZulu homeland in the 1970s, Zwelethini's ambition to play an independent political role brough him into direct conflict with his uncle, the Chief Minister. After attending a meeting called to discuss the formation of an opposition group to Inkatha, Zwelethini was hauled before the KwaZulu Legislative Assembly in 1976, dressed down and required to sign an oath which barred the king not just from party politics but from political activity of any kind. Three years later, accused of breaking his vow, he was summoned again before the KwaZulu Legislative

Assembly where Buthelezi spent a whole afternoon heaping rebukes on him. Unable to contain his distress, the king jumped up and ran out of the chamber. He later likened himself to King Duncan in Shakespeare's *Macbeth*. Buthelezi remarked at the time: 'It is not proper for us to drag our king into the political games that we play.' Now facing the greatest challenge of his life, Buthelezi was only too willing to drag the king into his own political games.

The position of the king had hitherto not merited special attention. Neither de Klerk nor Mandela had difficulty in principle with the idea of ensuring him a special constitutional role in KwaZulu/Natal if he wanted one. But the king's status now became the central part of Buthelezi's strategy, on which he was to make his final stand. The initial issue which helped galvanise the king was the removal of the name of KwaZulu from the map of South Africa. This, he said in a memorandum to de Klerk in January, rendered the new constitution 'so alien' that he felt obliged to reject it. 'It amounts to the expunging of the very name of my kingdom from the constitution of South Africa. We cannot, therefore, be expected to regard it as our constitution. This has sent shock waves throughout the psyche of every one of our Zulu subjects.'

As the struggle intensified, so did the king's demands. In a meeting with de Klerk in February, Zwelethini demanded a sovereign Zulu kingdom encompassing the whole of Natal, restoring what he claimed were its boundaries in the 1830s, before the era of white conquest. 'I am asking for something that belongs to me and my people – no one else.' In public speeches, he now followed the same rhetoric as Buthelezi. 'I will die rather than insult the memory of my great ancestral kings by handing over the land of their people to our political enemies.' He duly rejected the interim constitution and declared he would not abide by the election results.

The extent of Zwelethini's territorial claims was questionable. The Zulu kingdom had come into existence in the 1820s as an amalgamation of independent chiefdoms in what later became the northern half of Natal. After its defeat by British forces in 1879 and a subsequent civil war amongst the Zulu people, the kingdom had been all but destroyed and incorporated into the colony of Natal. The status of the king had been reduced to that of a paramount chief. It was only the apartheid system which had created KwaZulu from an archipelago of nearly 50 pieces of territory and which enabled the king to regain his status.

Nevertheless, allegiance to the Zulu king was far more widespread amongst Zulus than any loyalty to Inkatha. Opinion polls suggested that he was the most popular leader among blacks in Natal. As a rallying point for Zulu nationalists, therefore, the king carried far more influence than Buthelezi on his own could muster. But the risks for the monarchy itself were considerable. By becoming overtly involved in political issues which were already causing deep divisions among the Zulu people, Zwelethini endangered the unifying role that the Zulu monarchy had traditionally played. As opinion polls also showed, Buthelezi's own popularity had suffered as a result of his belligerent boycotts over constitutional negotiations and his dubious alliance with white extremists; in Natal, Inkatha collected less than one quarter of the vote and, on a national basis, less than five per cent. A clear majority of the region's population were said to favour KwaZulu/Natal's continued involvement as a province of South Africa. By linking himself to Buthelezi's fortunes, the king risked a similar fate for the Zulu monarchy. The Zulu-speaking journalist, Mondli waka Makhanya, warned in the Johannesburg *Weekly Mail*: 'If His Majesty broke free of the leash his uncle Mangosuthu Buthelezi has placed around his neck and ventured beyond his palace gates, he would weep on hearing the ridicule many of his subjects now heap on him. Millions of Zulu-speaking people – especially those who have suffered untold woe from the violence racking Natal – now despise him for not acting authoritatively to prevent the disintegration of the nation and choosing to toe the line of the party that pays his bill.'

In the far-right camp, the mood of anger and resentment at what many Afrikaners considered to be de Klerk's capitulation to and appeasement of black aspirations also became more intense as each day brought closer the prospect of an ANC-dominated government. Demands for a *volkstaat* were frequently accompanied by threats of violence. 'Mandela, give us a *volkstaat* or you'll have total war in South Africa,' the extremist leader, Terre'Blanche, told supporters at Lichtenburg. A spate of bomb explosions on railway tracks, power pylons and ANC property in the Transvaal and the Orange Free State underlined the message.

Yet for all the fervour that was felt over the issue of a *volkstaat*, far-right parties, after four years of talk, still failed to explain where it would be located or how it would work. Road signs decorated with the flags of the old Boer republics were hoisted at the entrance to many *platteland* towns, declaring their allegiance to a *volkstaat*. But there was not one magisterial district in South Africa where whites constituted a majority of inhabitants, and no explanation was forthcoming about the rights of non-Afrikaners living in an area to be declared a *volkstaat*, nor of how their reactions would be taken into account. De Klerk described the idea as 'a hopeless illusion'.

The ANC nevertheless took far more seriously threats emanating from far-right parties than from Inkatha and acted towards them in a more conciliatory manner. 'The ultra-right is powerful in the proper sense of the word,' said Mandela in January 1994. They had significant support in the public service, the army, the police and other strategic institutions. 'They are trained and experienced and they know the country better than we do ... They can derail any democratic government in this country.'

Mandela was encouraged by the moderate approach adopted by the AVF leader, General Viljoen, whose own experience of warfare in Angola, Mozambique and Namibia had led him to conclude that violence was the worst possible option. In talks with Viljoen, ANC negotiators agreed that if the AVF participated in the election, its vote would be taken as an indication of support for a *volkstaat* and used as the basis to establish an Afrikaner council which would pursue the idea further. But in trying to sell this proposal to an AVF meeting in February, Viljoen was shouted down and denounced as a 'traitor' and 'coward'. The crowd favoured Terre'Blanche's approach.

By the time the first official deadline for registration of parties had been reached on February 12, the four key members of the Freedom Alliance – Inkatha, the AVF, the Conservative Party and Bophuthatswana – were all standing firmly against participation in the election. Only Ciskei, whose military dictator, Brigadier Gqozo, had succumbed to pressure from his own troops worried about their career prospects, had thrown in its hand. Whereas this prospect had not given the ANC any undue cause for alarm back in December, by February, after a series of security briefings and an outpouring of public concern about the ANC's intransigence, Mandela was ready to make the kind of compromises he had previously spurned, in an attempt to draw the Freedom Alliance into the constitutional process.

Security concerns were a particularly influential factor. Not only did intelligence reports indicate that right-wing groups were making serious preparations for resistance, stockpiling weapons, ammunition and medical supplies and organising training, but they raised questions about the loyalty of security force elements that might be required to deal with right-wing threats at the behest of an ANC-dominated government. The assessment of the government was that everything possible had to be done to avoid any kind of confrontation that would enable the alliance to make a common stand, drawing large numbers of their followers into the fray.

Mandela's concessions, announced unconditionally on

February 16, endorsed by the government and subsequently passed by parliament as constitutional amendments, went a long way towards meeting the demands set out by the Freedom Alliance in December. They included the use of a double ballot for provincial and national elections; wider powers for provincial government, including limited taxation powers; and guarantees that provincial powers would not be substantially diminished when the constituent assembly drafted the final constitution. The province of Natal would be renamed KwaZulu/Natal; a principle of 'internal' self-determination for groups sharing a common cultural and language heritage would be included in the constitution to meet the anxieties of both Zulu and Afrikaner nationalists; and the issue of a *volkstaat* would be dealt with by authorising the establishment of a 20-member council, to be elected by MPs who supported the establishment of a *volkstaat*, enabling the idea to be pursued by constitutional means.

Within hours, without waiting to consult his colleagues in the Freedom Alliance, Buthelezi dismissed the concessions as nothing more than 'cheap politicking', adding, 'Mr Mandela's supposed concessions do not even begin to address our demands.' But Buthelezi's abrupt rejection of the offer – sending facsimiles to newspaper offices in the early hours of the morning – not only reinforced suspicions that he had no intention at all of participating in the elections for fear of what it would reveal about the level of his support, but placed him at odds with other members of the Freedom Alliance who wanted a more considered response. General Viljoen, for one, was ready to accept the inclusion of a principle of self-determination and a *volkstaat* council as a reasonable basis for agreeing to participate in the election, even if other AVF leaders were not. Bophuthatswana's negotiators, concerned about a wave of strikes by public sector workers restless about their future after the election and the fate of their pensions, were also looking for an accommodation.

The approach of deadlines – real deadlines – concentrated everyone's attention. To keep the electoral process on course, the Independent Electoral Commission imposed a final deadline of March 4 for political parties to register, so that they could be included on the ballot paper. A further short period would be allowed after that date for political parties to present their list of candidates, thereby effectively confirming their participation in the election. The deadline set for that, eventually, was March 11. Beyond that, there would be no further leeway possible if the ballot papers were to be printed and distributed in time for an April 27 election.

The registration of parties was of more than ordinary significance. In the case of Bophuthatswana and KwaZulu, it meant that homeland governments there would be committed to ensuring free political activity in their areas. So far, the only political activity permitted in Bophuthatswana by its dictatorial president, Lucas Mangope, had been confined to his ruling Christian Democratic Party. Other parties, like the ANC, endeavouring to campaign in Bophuthatswana, had been blocked by police action. Even National Party officials had been harassed. Voter education workshops had been declared illegal gatherings and their participants brutally assaulted. By registering his party for the election, Mangope would be obliged to allow other parties to enter his territory to campaign. The same commitment would have to be made by Buthelezi in KwaZulu if Inkatha registered.

In a final effort to bring Inkatha into the election, Mandela arranged to meet Buthelezi in Durban on March 1, telling a political rally in advance: 'I will go down on my knees to beg those who want to drag our country into bloodshed and to persuade them not to do so.' The meeting was only their fourth encounter in the four years since Mandela's release from prison. It brought no movement on the constitutional dispute. But what it did produce was a deal of minor significance which was to have profound repercussions. In exchange for Mandela's agreement to put their constitutional differences to international mediation – a device which Buthelezi hoped would postpone the election altogether – Buthelezi agreed to register Inkatha for the election, 'provisionally'.

This agreement, reached with only three days left before the registration deadline, threw Buthelezi's allies in the Freedom Alliance into turmoil, with rival groups within each party arguing over the options they now faced. By the time the deadline of midnight on March 4 arrived, the Conservative Party, the Afrikaner Volksfront and Mangope's Christian Democratic Party had all decided against registration and to reject participation in the election.

But with only minutes to spare, after an evening of frantic activity, having heard on the radio that Inkatha had gone ahead and registered 'provisionally', General Viljoen, accompanied by his fellow retired generals in the AVF, arrived at the registration office to enlist a new party, Vryheids Front (Freedom Front), to keep open the possibility of right-wing participation in the election. The generals had chosen to register a party under that name because they had had no time beforehand to consult with other AVF leaders. The following day, Viljoen was vilified for his action at a meeting of the AVF which voted overwhelmingly to let the registration lapse.

The ground on which members of the Freedom Alliance had made their stand now began to give way. Mangope was the first victim. Accustomed to ruling Bophuthatswana with an iron rod and to relying on police to silence opponents, he had little regard for the groundswell of anger among civil servants and other public sector workers worried about their pensions and the uncertain prospects that Bophuthatswana faced. His one-party state system, with control of radio, television and parliament, gave him no insight into the popular pressures building up. Opinion polls suggested that Mangope had minimal public support – less than one per cent – but this had never before caused him any concern in all his time as ruler of Bophuthatswana, since 1977. At the previous election, in October 1992, all government candidates had been returned – unopposed.

Mangope's belief in tight discipline and control had made him an ideal partner in the apartheid system. He was far more reliable, more predictable, than Buthelezi. Whereas Buthelezi had refused 'independence', Mangope had taken it. When the South Africans came to rescue him from an attempted military coup in 1988, Mangope greeted the white minister who arrived on the scene with the words: 'Oh! I never knew how friends could be so loyal.' But none of this prepared him to cope either with the rapid change in political circumstance that Bophuthatswana faced, or with the change in outlook that his 'friends' in Pretoria had undergone.

Technically, under South African law, Bophuthatswana was still an independent state. At the same time, Bophuthatswana's adult population of two million had been given the right to vote in the April election as South African citizens. Once the election had taken place, the fate of Bophuthatswana was to be reincorporated into South Africa as a part of North West province.

By joining the Freedom Alliance, Mangope hoped to secure for Bophuthatswana and for himself a future in a federal system, though Pretoria's envoys, with whom he was now at odds, constantly warned him that this was an unlikely prospect. But by refusing to allow Bophuthatswana to participate in the election, when signs of popular unrest were already evident, when strikes were underway and when it seemed that even Buthelezi had signed up for the election, Mangope seemed oblivious to all political reality. His Pretoria friends were left baffled by what he hoped to achieve. 'I love him dearly but he is living in a different world,' reported South Africa's 'ambassador' to Bophuthatswana, Tjaart van der Walt. 'I failed to convey a sense of reality to him.' Mandela, in his conversations with Mangope, urging him to let the people of Bophuthatswana decide their future, also admitted failure.

'It seems I am talking to a stone. I think we have now given him enough time. I have tried to reason with him but it is clear he has no vision. Further pressures will be used and I have no doubt he will not be able to withstand them.'

Aided and abetted by ANC activists, the strikes spread through Bophuthatswana, affecting civil service departments, schools, telecommunications, health services, electricity supplies, transport and industry. Radio and television broadcasts went off the air. The demands of the strikers no longer centred just on pension payouts but included demands for Bophuthatswana's immediate reincorporation into South Africa, for free and fair elections and for Mangope's removal. On the streets of Mafikeng, running battles broke out between police and striking workers and students. All that stood between Mangope and popular revolt were his police and security forces.

Yet still Mangope refused to bend. When the head of the Independent Electoral Commission, Judge Johann Kriegler, met him in Mmabatho in March 9, seeking assistance in providing voting facilities in Bophuthatswana for South African citizens and in ensuring that free political activity could take place, Mangope responded with a flat rejection, even though tear-gas was filling the streets outside as police struggled to disperse protesting government employees. That same day he fired the staff of the Bophuthatswana Broadcasting Corporation, closing down two television stations and three radio stations.

The mood on the streets became increasingly ugly. Police found themselves the target of attack by activists. Some wavered, fraternising with the strikers. A group of dissident policemen delivered a memorandum to the South African 'embassy' supporting the demand for reincorporation and participation in the election. A government minister resigned saying he was tired of 'listening to a 70-year-old saying he would die for the sovereignty of the homeland'. Looters began to raid shopping centres.

Mangope's next action precipitated a crisis with such potential for disaster that it suggested he had lost touch with all reason. Fearing that revolution was imminent, Mangope met General Viljoen, his Freedom Alliance partner, pleading for help from armed white paramilitary forces in the extremist Afrikaner Volksfront. Viljoen promised to muster 3,000 men. A former commander of the disbanded 32 Battalion, Colonel Jan Breytenbach, was appointed to lead the AVF force. Learning of the instruction to mobilise, the AWB leader, Eugene Terre'Blanche, issued a call, broadcast on a right-wing radio station near Pretoria, for members of his *wenkommando* to report to its headquarters at Ventersdorp, a town in western Transvaal within striking distance of the Bophuthatswana capital. On the night of May 10, hundreds of AVF and AWB members, armed with an assortment of shotguns and hunting rifles, crossed into Bophuthatswana in convoys of pick-up trucks, assembling at Mmabatho air-force base. Many right-wingers believed they might be on the verge of establishing a *volkstaat*.

However, the arrival of the AWB, notorious for its lawless conduct and racist attacks on blacks, provoked immediate dissension, both with AVF leaders and with white officers in command of the small Bophuthatswana Defence Force. In a series of altercations, the BDF commander, General Jack Turner, ordered Terre'Blanche to take his men out of Bophuthatswana. The AVF leader, Colonel Breytenbach, also told him to get out. Forced eventually to go, AWB members went on what was described as 'a kaffir-shooting' expedition in the streets of Mmabatho, firing at random at bystanders and terrorising the local inhabitants. As they were pulling out, a vehicle carrying an AWB 'general' and two other men was caught in a gun-fight with government troops in the centre of Mmabatho. The 'general' was killed; his two companions survived but were executed by a policeman as they lay on the ground, in full view of television cameras. Later in the day, March 10, the AVF force retreated ignominiously out of Bophuthatswana.

Even now, with mayhem on the streets of his capital, Mangope still failed to comprehend the reality of his position. His appeal to white right-wingers had led to a murderous rampage among his own people; part of his police force had mutinied; three days of looting had caused massive damage to shopping centres; his administration had collapsed; strikes had paralysed the country; and South African troops had arrived in Mmabatho ready to intervene.

Yet still Mangope acted as though he possessed options. In a statement delivered to Pretoria on March 11, Mangope said he would agree to participate in the elections, provided certain conditions were met. His position was rejected by de Klerk. In the afternoon, after a period of dithering, Mangope announced that he would recommend to a special sitting of the Bophuthatswana parliament the following week that the homeland should take part in the election. But when Judge Kriegler returned to Mmabatho later that day to secure a commitment allowing free political activity, Mangope prevaricated once more, perhaps believing that the South African Defence Force would protect him as it had done before.

The following day, March 12, de Klerk, in conjunction with the Transitional Executive Council, resolved that Mangope would have to be deposed. A deputation to Mangope's luxurious house near Zeerust arrived late that night. The man given the task of telling him was the Foreign Minister, Pik Botha, who six years previously had been greeted so warmly by Mangope when rescuing him from an attempted *coup d'état*. Botha explained that it was time for Mangope to retire. Mangope tried to argue, but to no avail. Eventually, he said, 'I hear you. You have come to oust me.'

The events culminating in the coup in Bophuthatswana produced dramatic changes across the political landscape, shattering the Freedom Alliance and throwing the far-right into a frenzy of recrimination. Appalled by the fiasco of armed intervention in Bophuthatswana, Viljoen broke with the AVF and, with only minutes to spare before the deadline at midnight on March 11, lodged a list of Freedom Front candidates ready to participate in the election, providing a vital route for the far-right to remain in the political process. The AWB denounced him as 'a political Judas goat sent by the Broederbond-ANC-NP-Communist Party alliance to lead us to the slaughter'. Terre'Blanche claimed his men had scored a 'brilliant victory' in Bophuthatswana. But the reality was that the AWB had been shown up as nothing more than a demented rabble. Many Afrikaners were disgusted by his farcical boasting carried on in the name of the Afrikaner people. Fear of the extreme right gave way to ridicule.

While Viljoen took the gap, Buthelezi decided to close it, failing to register a list of candidates and isolating himself and Inkatha from the election process. It was a fateful decision. Buthelezi's only real option left, if he were to prevent the ANC from winning control of KwaZulu/Natal at the polls, was to stop the election taking place there, to enforce a delay in the hope that a more favourable deal might be obtained at a later stage, possibly through international mediation. The only means he possessed of doing this were either the threat of violence or the use of it. Yet both de Klerk and Mandela, acting in concert through the Transitional Executive Council, had shown with Bophuthatswana their joint determination to protect the election process from obstruction. Both were adamant that the election should proceed according to plan. Moreover, as the Bophuthatswana coup had also shown, the SADF was ready to support them.

Tremors from Bophuthatswana reverberated throughout the homeland system. The same fears over pensions and salaries led to protests by public servants in Lebowa, Transkei, Venda and Qwa Qwa. The most dramatic effect came in Ciskei. Its military dictator, Brigadier Gqozo, had broken with the Freedom Alliance in January and signed up for the election, hoping his African Democratic Party would secure him a place in the future. But faced with striking civil servants and rebellious police, all urged on by ANC activists, Gqozo capitulated on March 22, asking Pretoria to take over Ciskei's administration. 'I am relieved in a sense,' said Gqozo, shortly after standing down. 'Though I did not want this to happen, I have no option. I would not like to end up in a situation where the whole place is up in smoke.' South African troops once more moved in to secure control. 'Two down,' commented Joe Slovo, the SACP leader, gleefully, 'one more to go.'

The ensuing crisis in KwaZulu in 1994 was the culmination of a power struggle amongst the Zulu people which had begun nearly ten years before. Buthelezi's role in the apartheid system as a homeland leader had enabled him to entrench his position in KwaZulu with personal command of the government's apparatus. Since the mid-1970s, he had run KwaZulu as a one-party state, controlling its parliament, its police and civil service, brooking no opposition and intolerant of criticism. As a member of the Zulu royal family, he could rely on the support of a powerful network of Zulu traditional chiefs – *amakhosi* – whom he in turn rewarded with power and privilege. The Zulu system of loyalty and obedience to its hierarchy assured Buthelezi of bedrock support among more traditionally-minded communities, particularly those in the deep rural areas of KwaZulu. Migrant workers on the Witwatersrand, coming from those rural areas, bore him the same allegiance. Buthelezi's capital at Ulundi, a remote hilltop surrounded by rolling hills, cut off from the mainstream of political activity and entirely subservient to his leadership, served to reinforce the notion of his own power.

South Africa's white rulers were only too content to allow Buthelezi this degree of control. So much of the KwaZulu system he ran represented the embodiment of their dreams of 'grand' apartheid, the territorial separation of South Africa into white-ruled and black-ruled areas. They were particularly appreciative of his vociferous opposition to economic sanctions and to the use of violence to resolve political conflict in South Africa. Their only disappointment was that Buthelezi rejected offers of 'independence' which would have allowed him even greater power.

In meeting the challenge posed by pro-ANC activists in the mid-1980s, Buthelezi and the government found themselves making common cause. Buthelezi was given every encouragement to deal forcefully with the threat both officially and by covert means. In 1986, with black townships erupting in revolt, a group of 200 Inkatha members were taken to a base in the Caprivi Strip by the Department of Military Intelligence (DMI), for training in the use of weapons, interrogation and surveillance techniques and urban warfare tactics. They remained on the payroll of the DMI until 1989 when they were formally incorporated into the KwaZulu Police, which Buthelezi, as Minister of Police, controlled. According to the Goldstone Commission into political violence, these men were frequently used in hit-squad activities.

The unbanning of the ANC in 1990 led not to any attempt at reconciliation with them but to an escalating conflict. The ANC lost no time in identifying that Inkatha was its enemy as much as the white government. 'Isolate Buthelezi' was the strategy pursued. Mandela's advisers urged him to avoid any dealings with Buthelezi; a whole year passed before they were to meet. Determined to establish a centralised system of government in post-apartheid South Africa, the ANC was innately hostile to groups which wanted a federal or confederal system, giving them a wide measure of regional autonomy, precisely to prevent an ANC government from exercising centralised control. Inkatha was certainly the main obstacle. But the cost of attempting to 'isolate Buthelezi' was to be inordinately high.

Inkatha, meanwhile, continued to receive support from covert units in the police and security forces aiming to stoke up the fires of ethnic conflict and thwart the possibility of any settlement which would result in the ANC taking power. The evidence of 'third force' activity was at first limited, seized upon readily by the ANC and critics of the government, but lacking real substance. In February 1994, however, Judge Goldstone acquired 'convincing evidence' of what was later described as 'a horrible network of criminal activity' involving high-ranking police officers in Pretoria, Inkatha and the KwaZulu Police. This activity, according to Goldstone, included assassination, train massacres, hostel violence, gun-running and the subversion of justice. Factories in the Transvaal were used by a police covert unit to manufacture homemade guns, which, along with large quantities of other weapons, were smuggled to Inkatha and used in attacks in Natal and on the Reef. The Caprivi Strip graduates were deeply involved. Goldstone emphasised that only a small group within the South African police force were to blame. But he also revealed, without implicating Buthelezi personally, that the evidence reached into the office of the Chief Minister of KwaZulu.

While this kind of activity was underway, in the negotiations Buthelezi stuck steadfastly to his case for a federal constitution, recruiting right-wing American advisers to help him. The version of federalism which he proposed not only reduced the functions of central government to a minimum, they concentrated enormous power in the hands of the rulers of KwaZulu/Natal, with few checks and balances. Buthelezi played no direct part in the negotiations. But his all-or-nothing approach was duly kept up by one of his closest advisers, Walter Felgate, a white social anthropologist who became the epitome of Inkatha's intransigence. Another adviser on whom Buthelezi relied was Mario Ambrosini, an American lawyer who persistently tried to attend the negotiation proceedings in defiance of the ruling that foreigners were not eligible there. Buthelezi frequently listened more to the advice of such men than to other members of his retinue who suggested more conciliatory positions.

The case for a federal South Africa was eminently

respectable. It would have suited several minority groups. But whatever chances there were of obtaining a federal state during the course of negotiations were thrown away by Buthelezi himself. Believing that he was too important for the process to continue without him, he resorted to boycott in the expectation that his adversaries would eventually be obliged to meet his demands. Even his advisers conceded that Buthelezi's ego was a significant aspect of the problem. His boycott did eventually succeed in producing concessions from Mandela which were widely welcomed. But Buthelezi saw fit to dismiss them out of hand, assuming that he could still gain more and hold up the process until he did so.

By then, his increasingly volatile behaviour, his belligerence, threats and posturing had alienated all his political allies, both in South Africa and abroad. His shabby alliance with white extremists and other homeland dictators attempting to thwart the electoral process had cost him much support. The irony of his position was striking. Once a willing participant under the apartheid constitution, he now rejected the new democratic one as being 'fatally flawed'. Once a firm opponent of boycotts and sanctions during the apartheid era, he now used boycotts as a principal weapon to disrupt South Africa's first democratic election. Once an ardent constitutionalist vociferously opposed to violence, he now used the threat of civil war to halt the constitutional process. But even more striking was the terminal nature of his strategy. By participating in the election, Buthelezi at least stood to gain a prominent position in KwaZulu/Natal or in national political life. If he failed to stop the election, the day afterwards he would not only lose control of all the official levers of power but leave his own followers unrepresented and his civil service facing an uncertain future under an ANC-dominated government. As election day approached, his hilltop capital of Ulundi was gripped by a siege mentality, rife with fear and apprehension.

ANC officials, sensing that another victory in the wake

of Bophuthatswana and Ciskei was imminent, continued to taunt Buthelezi, taking courage from opinion polls which suggested that in KwaZulu/Natal support for the ANC was greater than for Inkatha. Ramaphosa spoke recklessly of the need for a military solution, having no concept of what it involved. Slovo predicted that Buthelezi would be 'merely a smell in history' after the election, claiming that he himself, a non-Zulu, could get more votes in KwaZulu/Natal than Buthelezi. Both exemplified the arrogant and aggressive face of the ANC which many of its opponents feared would become a feature of life after the election. For those in Ulundi the message was all too clear: the ANC wanted to smash KwaZulu, destroy its king and break for ever the Zulu nation.

Yet Buthelezi's power base was far stronger than the glib pronouncements of ANC politicians suggested. Buthelezi had worked hard since the 1970s to re-establish the sense of a Zulu nation. In the rural backwaters of KwaZulu/Natal lived several million Zulus ready to obey the command of their traditional chiefs – *amakhosi* – and their king. Even though the Zulu people as a whole, some eight million in all, were deeply divided into rival camps supporting either Inkatha or the ANC, the position of the king exerted a profound influence over most of them. And, as the power struggle between Buthelezi and the ANC reached its peak, it was on the king that Buthelezi gambled his future.

In a prepared speech given in Ulundi on March 18, Zwelethini proclaimed a sovereign kingdom. 'We are here today to proclaim before the world, our freedom and sovereignty and our unwavering will to defend it at all costs,' he said. 'I call on all Zulus to fulfil their sacred duty to defend our freedom and sovereignty to anyone in Southern Africa who dares to challenge it.' He described elections under the interim constitution as 'an immediate denial of our claim for sovereignty and self-determination', and suggested Zulus should refrain from voting. 'I find it quite impossible to recommend that any of my subjects who are loyal to the throne should participate in the forthcoming election, unless this matter [a sovereign Zulu kingdom] is settled.'

On the ground, the conflict in KwaZulu/Natal grew ever more deadly. Election activity of any kind became a dangerous business in many areas, even for those engaged in voter education workshops, administrative tasks or peace-broking efforts. In February, in a southern Natal village previously untouched by political violence, a group of 15 ANC activists, after putting up posters offering 'Jobs, Peace, Freedom', were shot and hacked to death. 'The idea,' said a local peace committee chairman, 'is to instil maximum fear in those communities which are on the verge of making a political decision and to intimidate them from voting.' In Ulundi, a pamphlet was circulated naming 21 Inkatha leaders as secret ANC supporters. Two people on the list, a dissident prince in the royal family and a college registrar, were murdered. The level of intimidation from both camps soared by the day. 'Vote?' said a retired schoolteacher in Port Shepstone, 'Why vote? Inkatha is killing us, the ANC is killing us. We are all going to die.'

In mid-March, Inkatha supporters occupied the King Zwelethini stadium in Umlazi, near Durban, where an ANC rally was due to be held, on the grounds that it 'belongs to the king'. A week later, Inkatha blocked an ANC rally from taking place in the Princess Magogo stadium in KwaMashu, near Durban. The level of rhetoric, meanwhile, was raised to a new pitch. Buthelezi spoke of a 'fight to the finish' and 'a struggle for liberation from African National Congress/National Party oppression which will have no parallel in Africa'.

When Judge Kriegler, head of the Independent Electoral Commission (IEC), visited Ulundi to address the KwaZulu Legislative Assembly on March 23 in order to appeal for co-operation to ensure a free and fair election, he was repeatedly jeered. In response to Kriegler's list of requests for assistance, Buthelezi offered to make government school buildings available, but not community school buildings. Other government buildings, he said, would be made available provided they were not needed for 'essential services'. He also laid down conditions for co-operation from civil servants, loudly applauded by KwaZulu delegates. Those who wished to man polling stations would be allowed to do so, he said, provided that they were not involved in 'essential services', provided that the danger to them was spelt out and provided they were made aware that the KwaZulu government would not accept any liability for anything that happened to them.

In his report to de Klerk and Mandela delivered the following day, Kriegler described the event as 'stage-managed to humiliate the IEC'. His verdict was that without direct political intervention, free elections would be frustrated. 'In order for the IEC to conduct free and fair elections in KwaZulu/Natal, the requisite degree of stability and co-operation has to be established in the province as a matter of urgency.' He later spoke of his determination to mount the election in KwaZulu/Natal to show that 'spoilers cannot spoil the whole of the game'.

To demonstrate its own strength in KwaZulu/Natal, the ANC proposed a campaign of mass action there. Despite fears of violence erupting, an ANC march through the city centre in Durban on March 25 passed off relatively peacefully. Inkatha then decided to respond in kind in Johannesburg, but with calamitous results.

On March 28, thousands of Zulus, brandishing spears, clubs and cowhide shields, marched through the streets of the city's main business district to a rally at Library Gardens in support of Zwelethini's proclamation of a Zulu kingdom. The demonstration turned into a bloodbath when snipers opened fire from nearby buildings. For several hours, as Zulus went on the rampage, the streets in the city centre were scenes of chaos. At the ANC's headquarters at Shell House, ANC security guards shot and killed eight protesters who they said were trying to storm the building. By the end of the day, 53 people were dead, most of them demonstrators.

The spectacle of central Johannesburg being turned into a war zone set off a wave of alarm throughout South Africa and far beyond its borders. It was a time when confidence in the transition and the ability of South Africa's politicians to manage it successfully was grievously undermined at home and abroad. In anticipation of further violence, a surge of stockpiling began – canned food, candles, primus stoves, toilet paper, guns and ammunition. Talk of civil war became commonplace. Foreign investors too lost faith, withdrawing funds, shelving plans.

The event also tarnished Mandela's reputation. In the aftermath of the shootings outside the ANC's headquarters, Mandela personally prevented police who arrived with a search warrant from entering the building. Asked later at a press conference if his law and order minister would allow political opponents to set conditions for police probes into criminal activity, he replied: 'Let's face that when we are the government. I am entitled to negotiate with law and order officials.' The Johannesburg newspaper, the *Sunday Times*, observed caustically: 'What a rare achievement for the ANC. It has succeeded in putting itself above the law *before* taking power. In most banana republics it happens the other way around.'

The need for an initiative on KwaZulu/Natal was imperative. Not only was Judge Kriegler demanding one, but intelligence officials warned of a rapidly deteriorating security position there. Under the auspices of the KwaZulu government, 'self-protection units' were being armed and trained in rural camps with the aim of 'resistance' in mind. They had the reputation of being no more than a rag-tag army, known derisively as the 'five-rand brigade', the sum of money which each homeland resident was encouraged to donate to underwrite them. The numbers trained so far amounted to only about

5,000 men and women. The arms available to them were limited. But the clear intention was to lay the foundations for guerrilla warfare. The Self Protection Unit commander, Philip Powell, a former police intelligence officer, spoke openly of preparing for an underground struggle against the ANC. 'You don't need masses of sophisticated armaments,' he said. 'Vietnam was won by people on bicycles who made their own grenades.' Linked to the self-protection units were a variety of extremist white commando groups. Buthelezi, moreover, still had the support of the KwaZulu Police. His capacity to mobilise violent opposition to the election process in KwaZulu/Natal, given the king's position, the role of the *amakhosi*, and his control of the KwaZulu administration, was all too evident. In those circumstances, the ANC's plans for mass action were merely a recipe for disaster.

The military options were limited. The defence and police forces were far superior in strength to any militia that Inkatha could raise, but their resources were already stretched. The only readily available extra trained manpower were white reserves, members of the Citizen Force, many of whom would be reluctant to become involved in what had become a Zulu civil war. The crowded periurban settlements of KwaZulu/Natal were difficult enough to control even in times of stability. An area like Umlazi, outside Durban, contained two million blacks living in a bewildering maze of squatters' shacks, hostels and small homes spread over 30 square miles. Each section had its own dominant headman, warlord, gang leader or committee chairman. Boundaries between rival groups were rarely discernible to outsiders. The terrain of the rural areas beyond was mostly rolling hills and valleys where roads were poor and villages and kraals scattered and remote. Trying to pacify a tribally-based insurgency in this terrain was beyond the resources of the security forces. Nor did the military have the capacity to take control of Buthelezi's administration in Ulundi without starting a revolt.

The political options were also limited. Buthelezi's aim was to force a postponement of the election and then extract greater regional powers for KwaZulu/Natal, or, failing that, to ensure that the election was disrupted to such an extent that the result would not be regarded as legitimate, thereby keeping him at centre-stage. The missing link in this strategy was that, even if he succeeded in gaining greater regional powers for KwaZulu/Natal, the polls suggested he would still lose the election.

Both de Klerk and Mandela were adamant that there would be no postponement of the election. Not only would this hand a major political victory to Buthelezi, rewarding months of boycott, belligerence and sheer obstruction, but it would set off an explosion of anger in other parts of the country expecting the polls to proceed as promised. There was also no guarantee that postponing the poll would result in Buthelezi's subsequent participation.

The difficulty was in ensuring that the poll in KwaZulu/Natal acquired sufficient legitimacy. KwaZulu alone possessed some 2.5 million voters, about 60 per cent of Natal's black voters and some twelve per cent of the national electorate, most of whom it seemed were unlikely to have an opportunity to vote even if they wanted to. The mere act of voting, of being seen to vote, of walking in the direction of a polling station, could carry the risk of death or arson. Similar intimidation could be applied to those who did not want to vote. The problem was made worse by the carnage on the streets of Johannesburg, which confirmed to many Zulus in KwaZulu/Natal that they really were under attack and which set Buthelezi off on another round of wild rhetoric. 'The Shell House massacre,' declared Buthelezi, 'shows that we have now entered a final struggle to the finish between the ANC and the Zulu nation', and this could only be stopped, he claimed, if the election were postponed. The only hope that de Klerk and Mandela had for defusing the crisis was to prise King Zwelethini away from Buthelezi with guarantees of a constitutional role in the new order.

As a signal of their determination to keep the election on course, de Klerk declared on March 31 a state of emergency in KwaZulu/Natal. The practical effect was limited. Initially, only 2,000 extra troops were mobilised mainly to patrol black townships, an insignificant number given the overall scale of the problem. Emergency powers were used principally in the search for weapons. But it served as a timely warning to Buthelezi of the risks he was running.

An ill-tempered summit between de Klerk, Mandela, Buthelezi and Zwelethini at a lodge in the Kruger National Park on April 8 resolved nothing. Mandela arrived bearing a proposal offering to entrench the Zulu monarchy, with constitutional powers, prerogatives, rights and obligations, in the new constitution of KwaZulu/Natal and to provide it with a royal constabulary and a budget, giving the king a status not even accorded him under the KwaZulu constitution. The condition Mandela wanted for all this was that the king would undertake to do everything in his power 'to ensure that all persons seeking to participate and vote in the forthcoming elections shall be able to do so without hindrance'. He hoped to be able to speak to Zwelethini privately in advance of formal discussions.

But Buthelezi scuppered any such possibility, insisting that the king was accompanied by his full delegation. Before Mandela had an opportunity to put forward his proposal, Zwelethini read out a prepared statement as hostile, belligerent and as partisan as anything that Buthelezi might have made. He opened with a scathing attack on the ANC for the deaths which had occurred outside Shell House in Johannesburg and demanded that Mandela personally distance himself from the shedding of 'innocent blood of my father's people'. He lashed out at the state of emergency calling it 'an invasion ... an act of foreign aggression ... a rape of our national dignity and pride'. He and his people would never recognise the legitimacy of actions taken under the emergency. And he demanded once again the restoration of his kingdom.

The rest of the summit was predictable. Buthelezi reiterated his demand for a postponement of the election, linking it to any movement on the issue of the king's status. Mandela rejected any postponement: 'That day is sacrosanct,' he said. The only item that they could agree on was to allow international mediation to proceed.

Efforts at international mediation, however, soon degenerated into farce. The two main mediators, the former US Secretary of State, Henry Kissinger, and the former British Foreign Secretary, Lord Carrington, agreed to assist provided that the ANC and Inkatha first sorted out the terms of reference for mediation. Duly informed that the two parties had reached agreement on the terms of reference, they, and five other eminent men, travelled to South Africa only to find that no such agreement had been reached. Buthelezi wanted mediation to include the election date; the ANC did not. The mediators promptly left.

The failure of international mediation, however, left Buthelezi completely isolated, facing a king who, having considered Mandela's offer on the Zulu monarchy, was willing to accept it; a party rumbling with discontent at the prospect of being denied a legitimate place in the future; a civil service deeply worried about salaries and pensions; and a following only too eager to participate in the election. For Buthelezi himself, a future in the wilderness was not appealing.

Within days Buthelezi capitulated, using an itinerant Kenyan political consultant who had been attached to the mediation effort as an intermediary with de Klerk and Mandela. On April 19, with only seven days remaining, Buthelezi accepted the offer of a constitutional role for the Zulu monarchy and abandoned all his other demands.

His critics were quick to point out that since his decision in March to boycott the election some 700 lives had been lost in political violence. The comment of his hardline adviser, Walter Felgate, was that 'millions of rands' could not have bought the party the kind of media publicity it had received from boycotting the election process.

Chapter 6

The Interim Constitution

The new constitution marked the end of 341 years of white rule begun when the Dutchman, Jan van Riebeeck, first set foot on the Cape of Good Hope in 1652, and it brought to a close the shameful history of modern apartheid. It was passed by parliament in Cape Town on 22 December 1993, but not without dissension. In the white House of Assembly, Conservative Party MPs argued that it excluded 'a whole bloc of South Africans' and made no provision 'for people who want to be free'. Standing to attention, they sang the Afrikaans anthem, *Die Stem van Suid-Afrika*, in protest. As parliament voted for its own demise, after 83 years in existence, de Klerk declared that the moment was 'not a funeral, but a birth'. South Africa, he said, had embarked on 'a new Great Trek into the future'.

The centrepiece of the constitution was a bicameral parliament consisting of a National Assembly with 400 members elected by proportional representation, 200 of whom would come from national party lists and 200 from regional party lists; and a Senate composed of ten members from each of nine provinces, elected by members of each provincial legislature. Members of the National Assembly would elect the president at its first sitting. Any party with at least 80 National Assembly seats – equivalent to 20 per cent of the national vote – would be entitled to nominate a deputy president. If only one party held 80 seats or more, the party holding the second-largest number of seats would also be entitled to nominate a deputy president.

The cabinet would be a government of national unity lasting five years in which each party with at least 20 National Assembly seats, having gained at least five per cent of the vote nationally, would be entitled to a number of portfolios proportionate to the number of seats which it held. It would consist of the president, deputy presidents and no more than 27 ministers. The president would allocate portfolios in consultation with party leaders. Cabinet decisions would be made by ordinary majority 'in a consensus-seeking spirit'.

The National Assembly and the Senate, sitting in joint session, would form a Constituent Assembly to draw up the final constitution within two years. Its decisions would require a two-thirds majority and it would be further constrained by a set of constitutional principles laid down in the interim constitution. If the Constituent Assembly could not agree on the final constitution by a two-thirds majority within two years of its first sitting, the constitution would be put to a referendum requiring a 60 per cent majority. If this was not achieved, the president would have to dissolve parliament and call a new general election before the process began again.

The 34 constitutional principles which the final constitution would have to enshrine included: a unitary state, multiparty democracy, provincial 'integrity', basic human rights, the independence of the judiciary, and the right of 'internal' self-determination for specific groups.

At provincial level, the four existing regions – Cape, Natal, Orange Free State and Transvaal – would be replaced by nine new provinces: Eastern Cape, Western Cape, Northern Cape, Orange Free State, KwaZulu/Natal, Northern Transvaal, Eastern Transvaal, North West, and the industrial heartland, Pretoria-Witwatersrand-Vereeniging (PWV).

Each province would have its own legislature, with between 30 and 100 members, depending on the size of the local electorate, elected by proportional representation. Each party gaining at least ten per cent of the seats would be entitled to nominate members to an Executive Council. The Executive Council would consist of a premier and not more than ten other members. Each legislature would be entitled to write a constitution for its province which would have to accord with principles governing the national constitution and to receive approval from two-thirds of its members.

The powers of the provinces covered 29 areas including: primary and secondary schooling; health services; housing; some police activities; roads; public transport; tourism; cultural affairs; trade and industrial promotion; welfare services; and language policy. Central government would retain wide powers to intervene in provincial affairs under certain circumstances. But no changes could be made to the boundaries, powers and functions of the provinces without the approval of the provincial legislatures. Any amendments to the powers of the provinces proposed by the Constituent Assembly, when drawing up the final constitution, would require the approval of the Senate with a two-thirds majority.

In terms of revenue, each province would be entitled to an equitable share of nationally collected revenue. This would include a percentage, fixed by parliament, of income tax collected within its boundaries and other allocations of national revenue. Provincial legislatures could raise levies and duties other than income tax or value-added tax, for example, on casinos, gambling and betting.

At local government level, a new structure of multiracial town and city councils would be installed in phases. As a concession to right-wing local associations, racial quotas would be allowed: white voters in existing municipalities would elect 30 per cent of seats; black rate and rent payers would elect another 30 per cent; and the remainder would be elected on a non-racial basis.

There would be a new South African Police Service,

which would function at both a national and provincial level. A national commissioner, appointed by the president, would appoint nine provincial commissioners. Provincial premiers would have the right to approve or veto these appointments.

Whatever changes were made to the public service, the vast legions of civil servants, police, defence force personnel and parastatal employees would be guaranteed job security and pension rights. But this would not preclude an aggressive programme of affirmative action.

Other constitutional mechanisms included: a Bill of Rights; a Constitutional Court with final jurisdiction over the interpretation, protection and enforcement of the interim constitution; an Office of the Public Protector empowered to investigate government maladministration, abuse or unjustifiable exercise of power; and a Human Rights Commission.

In the interim period leading up to the elections in April 1994, a Transitional Executive Council (TEC), with members drawn from each party participating in the negotiation process, would be given wide powers to ensure the right conditions existed for free political participation and a free and fair election. The TEC would act as a check on government, the police, homeland administrations, military and paramilitary units and political parties in any area deemed to affect the election. It would be charged with eliminating impediments to legitimate political activity; ending intimidation that might affect the transition; and enabling all political parties to organise and canvass in all areas. Seven subcouncils would deal with law and order; stability and security; defence; intelligence; finance; foreign affairs; regional and local government and traditional authorities; and the status of women. Decisions on the TEC would be taken by consensus if possible, or else by three-quarters majority. These decisions would be binding on all governments, administrations and political parties whether or not they were participants in the Council. An appeal from TEC decisions could be lodged with a Special Electoral Court.

An Independent Electoral Commission (IEC), armed with extensive powers, would be responsible for the administration of the election, for voter education, for monitoring political campaigns and ensuring parties adhered to an electoral code of conduct. The IEC would have powers to move voting stations or even close them down during voting if it decided that a free and fair election in a particular area was rendered impossible as a result of intimidation or violence. It would also have powers, against which there would be no appeal, to disqualify all or some votes cast in an area and even to disqualify votes already cast in favour of any party. When the election was over, the IEC would have to decide whether the elections had been 'substantially free and fair'. Once this decision was made and announced, no other body in the country would have the legal power to challenge or overturn it. To assist it in this monumental task, the IEC would be supported by an Election Monitoring Directorate whose teams of monitors would observe and report all aspects of the campaign and electoral process and which would also be responsible, in conjunction with the police, for investigating irregularities, acting as peace-broker if necessary between rival parties, and issuing warnings over contraventions of the code of conduct.

An Independent Media Commission (IMC) would be charged with ensuring equitable treatment by broadcasting services of all political parties – a highly contentious area in view of the government's accustomed use of state-controlled radio for its own propaganda purposes. A broadcaster extending coverage to the election would have to provide 'reasonable opportunities' for discussion of conflicting views. Contraventions of IMC regulations would have to be rectified in further broadcasts; in more serious cases, fines or closure would be enforced. Party election broadcasts and political advertisements would be allowed only on public radio under strict control, but not on television.

Finally, a National Peace-keeping Force (NPKF), drawn from various police and military formations, would be established at short notice and deployed for public-order policing duties in an attempt to contain political violence. It was hoped that the NPKF would have greater credibility in township areas where the role of the police paramilitary force, the Internal Stability Division, was controversial.

Considering that four years previously South Africa had been in the hands of an authoritarian government, determined to protect white power and privilege, buttressed by a powerful civil service, by police and defence forces, and with access to huge state revenues, and that the likely outcome of the negotiations process was that South Africa would be ruled by a radical liberation movement, still in the throes of converting itself from armed resistance and popular revolt, what had been achieved was little short of a negotiated revolution. The word 'miracle' was frequently used to describe the constitutional agreement. That it was made possible was due in large part to the foresight and courage of de Klerk and the exemplary lack of bitterness shown by Mandela emerging from 27 years' imprisonment. Both had different aims and objectives. Both had shown the leadership necessary to obtain compromises on which a settlement could be based.

It was de Klerk who had travelled the greater distance. He had started out as a passionate advocate of group rights, of group self-determination. Indeed, even after the new constitutional agreement was reached, he still argued that separate development for different ethnic groups as a constitutional option was morally justified. From group rights he moved on to the idea of power-sharing through an enforced coalition. He repeatedly insisted that the National Party would never surrender to 'simple majority rule', leaving the fate of the white minority in the hands of a non-racial electorate. It would demand a guaranteed share in power, whatever the outcome of the popular vote, and it would hold out for as long as was necessary to obtain one. At the very least there would have to be a white veto in cabinet. De Klerk's strategy was based on the assumption that his government enjoyed such a preponderance of power that it could set the terms of any settlement.

The coalition deal that he eventually settled for was a workable, even an honourable settlement. He managed to secure guarantees on employment and pensions for the white establishment, and legal protection for white property and wealth. He also felt certain that in practice the indispensable role played by whites in the civil service, the security forces and the economy would provide the National Party, as the representative of their interests, with far more leverage over a new government than mere constitutional clauses. But all this was still a far cry from what he had in mind when he released Mandela in 1990 and indeed from the promises he made to the white electorate during the referendum campaign in 1992. As the remains of white power drained away at the end of the negotiations in November 1992, de Klerk, unable to put up further resistance, even abandoned his demand that cabinet decisions be taken by a two-thirds majority, potentially a means of minority veto, agreeing instead that they should be made within 'the consensus-seeking spirit' of the negotiating process. In a final encounter, Mandela insisted that power would be shared voluntarily or not at all.

Mandela embarked on the negotiations with the aim of achieving unfettered majority rule in the shortest possible time. He assumed that the government's vulnerability to international pressure, popular unrest and economic disruption, the very factors which he believed had led de Klerk to release him and lift the ban on the ANC in the first place, would work to his advantage in securing a speedy victory. The cordial nature of his early talks with de Klerk provided further evidence of the government's apparent flexibility. When de Klerk turned out to be a far tougher proposition than expected and ANC negotiators found themselves being drawn into making concessions far removed from those which party supporters were likely to accept, the surprise and shock for Mandela was all the greater. The National Party, he complained angrily 'keeps looking for ways to exercise power even if it loses a democratic election'. Yet in order to break the deadlock following the collapse of Codesa 2, Mandela had agreed to the idea of a 'sunset' clause offering the National Party a guaranteed role in a future coalition government, thereby providing the white community with reassurance about its political future, but delaying for a period of five years 'full' majority rule upon which he had put so much store. Moreover, Mandela had set out with plans for a strong centralised government, yet he had been obliged to give way to demands for a form of federal arrangement. And at local government level, to minimise the possibility of right-wing obstruction, he conceded to whites a minimum of 30 per cent representation on all town and city councils, a racial quota well beyond that which whites would otherwise obtain.

The cost of this long war of attrition in personal terms was considerable. Long gone were the days of the 'special relationship' when Mandela happily acknowledged de Klerk as a 'man of integrity'. In public and in private the relationship had become notably abrasive, particularly over the issue of violence. With each new piece of evidence of dirty tricks by security forces, Mandela became ever more convinced of the government's bad faith, accusing de Klerk of 'talking peace while ... conducting a war against us'. The township violence he also blamed on the government, claiming that de Klerk was indifferent to the loss of black lives. What also irked Mandela was de Klerk's persistent refusal to condemn the principle of apartheid. While de Klerk was willing to admit that the apartheid system had led to injustice and hardship, particularly the policy of forced removals, for which he apologised, he still continued to speak approvingly of the idea of ethnic separation providing it was voluntary. In heated moments, Mandela labelled de Klerk's government 'political animals', and 'an illegitimate, discredited minority regime'. When communications were broken off in 1992, in the wake of the Boipatong massacre, it was left to their two understudies, Roelf Meyer and Cyril Ramaphosa, the chief negotiators at the talks, to keep in contact privately to repair the link. Even on the occasion when the two men were jointly awarded the Nobel Peace Prize in Oslo in December 1993, the friction was still evident. In interviews, Mandela spoke of his 'disappointment' with de Klerk's conduct in the negotiations and once more accused the government of involvement in township violence. De Klerk, for his part, appeared to resent being upstaged by Mandela, believing that his own efforts had been overlooked. In choosing them as 'Men of the Year' for 1993, *Time* magazine noted that 'the mutual bitterness and resentments between de Klerk and Mandela are palpable'; and it asked rhetorically: 'How could these two have agreed on anything – lunch, for instance, much less the remaking of a nation?'

In quieter moments, Mandela acknowledged both the contribution that de Klerk had made to the transformation of South Africa from an apartheid state to a non-racial society and the difficulties he had faced in doing so. In the dark months of late 1992, when everything seemed to be falling apart, Mandela, at his home in the northern suburbs of Johannesburg, recalled a phone conversation he had recently had with de Klerk. 'I must say he sounded a bit down. He is a very brave chap, you know, very bright and confident, and it was worrying to hear him sounding so down.' In the hurlyburly of South African politics, the quieter moments were soon forgotten.

As for the interim constitution, it was essentially a deal between two parties, the National Party and the African National Congress, both of which had strong authoritarian tendencies, tempered only by what the small liberal

Democratic Party managed to insert and by the concessions made under pressure in February 1994 by Mandela in attempting to draw into the election process members of the Freedom Alliance. The National Party, a party of power and patronage, had more experience of suppressing human rights than of protecting them. The ANC's preoccupation was, simply, power. Issues of substance, like the 'six-pack' deal which initially decided on the use of a single ballot paper, were often thrashed out between the government and the ANC in secret meetings, then hurried through talks with only token debates and scant regard for the views of other parties.

Nothing illustrated better the hasty and secretive way in which significant aspects of the interim constitution were put together than the case of the Constitutional Court. The role of the Constitutional Court, consisting of a president and ten judges, was to be the watchdog of democracy, to ensure the protection of fundamental rights, to decide whether legislation accorded with those rights, and to determine whether the final constitution accorded with the set of constitutional principles laid out in the interim constitution. Appointments to the court were therefore of crucial importance. Late one Friday in November 1993, a few days before the final plenary session was due to adopt the bulk of the interim constitution, the government and the ANC announced an agreement which would have vested effective control of appointments to the court in the next government, ignoring a vigorous debate that had already taken place on the issue. The only time allowed for consideration of the matter was the following weekend as a decision was to be taken on the Monday. It took all the remaining fire-power that the Democratic Party could muster, in the face of jeering from opponents and snide interjections from the chair, to force a change towards a more independent method of selection.

Other deals arranged by the ANC and the National Party placed considerable power in the hands of party managers. The constitution required that members of parliament who resigned or were expelled from the party for which they were elected would be unseated and replaced by another nominee of that party. The effect was likely to be to stifle rigorous debate and dissent in the future.

The most crucial issue concerned the balance of power between central government and the provinces. For a wide range of minority communities, the main fear about the new political system was that it would offer them no choice of obtaining proper political representation or political power and cast them into the role of permanent opposition groups, enabling the central government to ignore minority interests and even to use its power to oppress them. Because the expected winner at the polls was the African National Congress, a party in favour of strong central government, with a record of advocating central economic planning and clear authoritarian tendencies, this fear was all the more pronounced. The ANC's argument that it needed a strong central government to carry out its essential task of ensuring that blacks, after centuries of deprivation, gained economic advancement, was reassuring to its own constituency, but left minority groups suspicious.

Demands for a federal system of government came from several quarters. The National Party, in its 1991 constitutional proposals, called for power to be divided between three tiers of government – central, provincial and local – with each tier having 'original and entrenched authority with which other tiers of government may not interfere'. The Democratic Party too favoured devolved powers. The most insistent of all was Inkatha. Buthelezi's plans for KwaZulu/Natal would have made it a semi-autonomous region. But having taken this stand, he then refused to participate in negotiations and threw away what chances there were, in alliance with the National Party and the Democratic Party, of obtaining greater federal powers in the constitution. His subsequent threats to boycott the election produced some further concessions from the

ANC, but left in place a constitution which allowed a strong degree of central government control.

Provinces, under the interim constitution, were given charge of 29 specific areas ranging from agriculture to welfare services. Provincial laws were to prevail over Acts of Parliament in these areas, except in specific cases. But the specific cases were defined in such a broad manner as to give central government ample scope for intervention. Central government was given overriding authority in cases where: provinces could not deal with a matter effectively; basic norms and standards were to be achieved and required national co-ordination and uniformity; necessary minimum standards were required for rendering public service; national intervention was required for the maintenance of economic unity, the protection of the environment, the promotion of interprovincial commerce, the protection of the common market in respect of the mobility of goods, services, capital or labour, or the maintenance of national security; or where provincial laws materially prejudiced the economic, health or security interests of another province or the country as a whole, or impeded the implementation of national economic policies. The provinces' powers of taxation, moreover, were of minor significance. What the constitution amounted to, in the words of one academic observer, was 'a basically unitary state with some federal fig leaves'.

Nevertheless, for all its defects, South Africa had acquired a workable constitution which opened the way to democracy. Its range of checks and balances was greater than anything that had preceded it. It was designed to last for only two years, while the final constitution was drawn up. There were hopes that, in that time, the defects might be rectified, that a better constitution might emerge. But that would depend upon the good intentions of politicians placed in power.

Chapter 7

Parties and Policies

African National Congress

In presenting itself to the electorate in 1994, the African National Congress possessed a unique pedigree. It had been in the business of fighting for political rights for more than 80 years, and its vision for the future from the start had been the kind of non-racial society which the country was on threshold of achieving, in large part through its own efforts.

The founders of the South African Native National Congress, as it was first called, were mostly conservative men – teachers, clergymen, clerks, journalists and businessmen – the products of missionary schools, influenced by Christian tradition and concerned largely with their own position in society. When they gathered in the city of Bloemfontein in January 1912, it was in response to the foundation of the Union of South Africa in 1910 which offered Africans virtually no prospect of political advancement. No Africans, Coloureds or Indians had been present at the deliberations of the National Convention which drew up the Union constitution; and no attention had been paid to the protests and petitions complaining about discrimination and their lack of rights. The principal aim of Britain, the colonial power, in forming the Union had been to forge new bonds, in the wake of the Anglo-Boer war, between the defeated Boer republics of the Transvaal and the Orange Free State and the British colonies of the Cape and Natal, not to involve itself with African interests. Only the Cape, where Coloureds and Africans had obtained limited voting rights, was prepared to defend their position. But Afrikaner politicians from the north made clear their determination to get rid of the African vote.

From the start, the ANC sought to unite Africans across tribal lines in dealing with the worsening plight they faced. By the turn of the twentieth century, after a series of wars and clashes against the British and the Boers lasting more than one hundred years, the African chiefdoms lying within South Africa had all succumbed to white rule. Most of their land had been acquired through conquest and settlement. Whole tribes had become resident on white-owned land where they worked as sharecroppers or labour tenants in exchange for a place to live, raise crops and pasture their cattle. Others were confined to areas designated as Native Reserves, patches of territory scattered throughout South Africa, numbering nearly 300 at the time, which had survived intact the era of white occupation. The reserves varied in size from a few square miles to large districts. In the Boer republics of the Transvaal and the Orange Free State only a tiny fraction of land had officially been set aside for Native Reserves, while in the Cape Colony and Natal, because of the military strength of Nguni chiefdoms like the Xhosa and Zulu, extensive areas remained under African control.

But African land occupation was soon under attack again. Following recommendations originally made by British administrators, the new Union government introduced, in 1913, the Natives' Land Act, intended to divide South Africa's land permanently between white and African areas. The Act prohibited Africans from purchasing or leasing land in white areas; henceforth the only areas where Africans could lawfully acquire land (outside the Cape) was in Native Reserves which then amounted to about eight per cent of the country. (This was later fixed at 13 per cent.) The effect of the Act was to uproot thousands of black tenants renting white-owned land -- 'squatters', as they were commonly known. Some sought refuge in the Reserves, although overcrowding there was already becoming a noticeable feature. Others were forced, after selling their livestock and implements, to work as labourers for white farmers. A whole class of prosperous peasant farmers was eventually destroyed. The impact was particularly severe in the Orange Free State where many white farmers lost no time in evicting 'squatters' in compliance with the law. The plight of these destitute families, driven off the land, was described by Sol Plaatje, the ANC's secretary, in his account of *Native Life in South Africa*. 'Awakening on Friday morning, 20 June 1913,' he wrote, 'the South African Native found himself not actually a slave, but a pariah in the land of his birth.' Plaatje recorded how, travelling through the Orange Free State in the winter of 1913, he found bands of African peasants trudging from one place to the next in search of a farmer who might give them shelter, their women and children shivering in the winter nights, their livestock emaciated and starving. 'It looks as if these people were so many fugitives escaping from a war.' The ANC sent a petition of protest to the prime minister in Cape Town and a delegation to Britain, but to no avail.

In the towns, the same process of segregation was applied. The towns had always been regarded as white preserves; Africans living there were treated as 'temporary sojourners', a convenient reservoir of labour needed for South Africa's growing industrial sector, but whose real homes were in the Reserves. This system was now enforced through a vast apparatus of controls, like pass laws. As housing was restricted, migrant labour hostels were commonly used to house male workers. In the job market, new labour policies excluded Africans from skilled and semi-skilled trades. By the 1920s, South Africa had developed an economic system allocating skills and high wages to whites and heavy labour and menial tasks to blacks on meagre pay. Remaining political rights were whittled away. In the 1930s, African voters were struck from the common roll in Cape Province, losing a right they had held for more than 80 years. At every turn, protests, petitions and polite deputations by the ANC proved fruitless. During the 1930s, the party fell into serious disarray. Twenty years of activity had rendered no advance.

A new generation of political activists emerged in the 1940s, contemptuous of the ANC for 'regarding itself as a body of gentlemen with clean hands' and determined to press for more forceful leadership. On Easter Sunday 1944, at the Bantu Men's Social Centre in Johannesburg, they formed the Congress Youth League, to act as an ANC pressure group, a 'brains trust' to give 'force, direction and vigour to the struggle for African National Freedom'. Among its founders were Nelson Mandela, who, after being expelled from Fort Hare University for participating in a student protest, was pursuing law studies in Johannesburg; Oliver Tambo, who had also been expelled from Fort Hare University as a result of a student strike and who was also studying law; and Walter Sisulu, a combative figure from rougher origins who had worked in factories, in the gold mines and in a series of labouring jobs, clashing repeatedly with whites over their racial attitudes. Most members were in their twenties, products of secondary schools and the University College of Fort Hare, now employed as teachers, articled clerks, journalists and trade unionists, all burning with ambition to establish a new nationalist ideology. 'We were never really young,' Oliver Tambo recalled. 'There were no dances, hardly a cinema, but meetings, discussions, every night, every weekend.'

The most heated debate centred on the question of whether one of the Youth League's aims should be 'to drive the white man into the sea'. The distrust of whites ran deep. Whites were not allowed to enlist as members of the African National Congress, partly for fear that they would seek to guide and control it for their own benefit.

Not even the help of white liberals was thought to be of use. There was an equally hostile attitude towards the Communist Party, a small but influential group which included whites and blacks as members. Distrusting the Communist Party's long-term commitment to a socialist revolution, the Youth League believed it would try to use the nationalist movement for its own ends and warned of 'the need for vigilance against communists and other groups which foster non-African interests'. Indian organisations were given similarly short shrift. At the heart of the Youth League's philosophy was a determination to assert an African identity, to give Africans control of their own future, to use African political power to change South African society. The African nationalist movement, said the Youth League, 'should be led by the Africans themselves'. But the extent to which other groups were to be excluded from the African struggle for power was an issue that was never resolved. At an early stage, two rival schools of thought emerged: the 'Africanist' school, which put African interests above all others; and the 'nationalist' school, which, wary of the dangers of developing an extremist black nationalism, preferred a more flexible approach towards other groups.

In drawing up its 'Basic Policy' in 1947, the Youth League endorsed more moderate thinking. 'It must be noted that there are two streams of African nationalism. One centres round Marcus Garvey's slogan "Africa for Africans". It is based on the "Quit Africa" slogan and the cry "Hurl the whiteman into the sea". This brand of African nationalism is extreme and ultra-revolutionary. There is another stream of African nationalism (Africanism) which is moderate, and which the Congress Youth League professes. We of the Youth League take account of the concrete situation in South Africa, and realise that the different racial groups have come to stay. But we insist that a condition for inter-racial peace and progress is the abandonment of white domination, and such a change in the basic structure of South African society that those relations which breed exploitation and human misery will disappear.' This division in African opinion was to be the cause of bitter clashes for years to come and endured into the 1990s.

With the advent of National Party rule in 1948 and the avalanche of apartheid legislation it brought, the young radicals of the Youth League began to recognise the need for a wider circle of allies. The best-organised anti-apartheid group was the Communist Party which had become increasingly effective in post-war years. Founded in 1921 by a group consisting mainly of foreign-born British radicals and Eastern European Jews, it had emerged from the Second World War with a small but efficient cadre of about 2,000 members – white, Indian, Coloured, but mainly African – who wielded considerable influence within multiracial trade unions and within the ANC and the South African Indian Congress. Communists played a major role in an African mine-workers' strike in 1946. They were active in township politics and they had the use of two communist-controlled newspapers. Three African communists were elected to the ANC's National Executive Committee in the late 1940s. The National Party government considered communism a 'national danger' and in 1950 introduced the Suppression of Communism Act, the first weapon in an arsenal of security measures acquired over the next four decades which eventually provided it with totalitarian control. But despite the banning of their party and their being the constant target of government attention, communists remained active within other organisations.

A change of leadership on the ANC National Executive in 1949 brought to the fore prominent members of the Youth League, including Mandela, Tambo and Sisulu, all the more determined to organise protest against the government. A 'Programme of Action' adopted in 1949 called for civil disobedience, boycotts and stay-at-home strikes on a mass scale. The objective now was 'national freedom', 'political independence' and 'self-determination'.

Joining forces with the South African Indian Congress (SAIC) and a Coloured protest group, the ANC launched the 'Defiance Campaign' in 1952. The plan was for groups of volunteers in major towns to flout apartheid laws with acts of defiance such as using railway coaches, waiting rooms and platform seats marked for Europeans only, by parading on the streets after curfew without permits, and by entering locations without permits. The idea was to fill the courts and prisons so they overflowed with petty offenders, thereby causing the system to break down. In five months, more than 8,000 people went to prison. The campaign eventually petered out, but it succeeded in transforming the ANC from an élite group into a mass movement.

Despite constant harassment from the government – police raids, surveillance, banning orders, restrictions, arrests, banishments and ever harsher security laws – the ANC persevered with plans for mass action. In 1953, it devised the idea of holding a 'Congress of the People', comprising delegates from every corner of the land, to draw up a new covenant, a 'Freedom Charter', and to indicate the road ahead towards a multiracial society. Support for the idea came from SAIC and from the South African Coloured People's Organisation based in Cape Town. Whites were also invited to participate. After initial misgivings, an enthusiastic response came from the Congress of Democrats, a small but influential group set up in 1953 by radical whites, many of them former members of the outlawed Communist Party. The multiracial South African Congress of Trade Unions also joined in.

The Congress of the People duly opened on 16 June 1955 on a bare stretch of ground near Kliptown, a ramshackle collection of houses and shacks ten miles to the south-west of Johannesburg. Some 3,000 delegates assembled – lawyers, doctors, clergymen, trade unionists, peasants and city workers – though several prominent ANC figures, like Mandela, were absent, forced to stay away by banning orders. Everywhere the ANC colours of black, green and yellow were on display. For two days the meeting continued with speeches, songs and hymns. The text of the Freedom Charter was read out, in English, Sesotho and Xhosa, and clause by clause approved by a show of hands. Towards the end of the second day, the police arrived in force, surrounded the meeting and announced that treason was suspected. They searched delegates, demanded their names, took photographs and confiscated documents, posters and banners. As they continued their work, the organisers resumed reading out the Freedom Charter to the crowd.

The Freedom Charter became the subject of endless controversy, yet it survived to influence successive generations of political activists and echoes from it could still be heard in the 1990s. Much of its content was relatively modest. The Freedom Charter affirmed the right of all citizens to vote, to hold office and be equal before the law. It promised equal status for 'all national groups' and an end to discriminatory legislation. It went on to declare that the mines, banks and 'monopoly' industries would be transferred into public ownership and that land would be redivided. Other promises concerned free compulsory education, minimum wages, free medical care, and welfare for the aged. The tone throughout was idealistic, at times naïve. 'Rent and prices shall be lowered, food plentiful and no one shall go hungry,' the Freedom Charter proclaimed. 'Slums shall be demolished, and new suburbs built.' No suggestions were put forward as to how all this would be achieved. In the South African context, however, such sentiments were dangerous. White liberals deplored the 'socialist' character of the Freedom Charter, arguing that left-wing activists in the Congress had clearly got the upper hand. The government deemed the Charter to be subversive. Mandela himself later acknowledged: 'It is a revolutionary document precisely because the changes it envisages cannot be won without breaking up the economic and political set-up of present South Africa.'

A new round of harassment began, culminating in the arrest on charges of high treason of 156 people. Among the accused were prominent ANC figures, like Mandela, Sisulu and Tambo, and white activists like the advocate Joe Slovo and his wife, Ruth First, both former members of the banned Communist Party. In all some 23 whites were put on trial. The prosecution asserted that the accused had been preparing 'for the overthrow of the existing State by revolutionary methods, involving violence and the establishment of the so-called People's Democracy', citing as its main evidence the Freedom Charter.

The Treason Trial gave the ANC greater prominence than ever before. For many blacks it meant that the ANC had emerged as a real force capable of challenging the government. Overnight the accused became popular heroes. The presence of so many whites on trial was seen by many blacks as evidence that whites too were beginning to turn against the government. ANC leaders, convinced that the handful of whites who supported them represented something more than a fringe of white politics, placed inordinate hope in the notion that eventually enough whites would have a change of heart about apartheid to bring about the downfall of the government. 'As far as the National Party is concerned,' wrote Sisulu in an article published in January 1957, 'any serious analysis will reveal that it has reached its high-water mark.'

It was a common failing of the ANC in the 1950s and 1960s continually to underestimate the strength and ruthlessness of South Africa's white rulers. In power was a government determined not only to curb dissent with whatever measures it deemed necessary but which, in its drive to secure a permanent solution to the problem of the *swart gevaar*, had set its sights on reconstructing South Africa on a scale that would involve upheaval and hardship for millions of its people. In such circumstances, the chances of survival for the ANC were slim, let alone its notion of bringing white rule to an end.

The Treason Trial was to drag on for more than four

years, sapping the energy of the movement and its leaders, before it was to end in their acquittal. Deprived of effective leadership, short of funds, poorly organised, the ANC fell into disarray. Other than mass protest, it had no coherent strategy. Disputes and dissension, never far below the surface, broke out anew, threatening to wreck the movement from within.

The Africanist wing had become increasingly critical of the direction taken by the ANC, in particular of its policy of seeking alliances with other racial groups. The rift had taken shape in the aftermath of the Defiance Campaign and it had widened when the ANC had joined forces with whites and Indians in the Congress Alliance during the preparations for the Congress of the People. The Africanists claimed that the ANC, by accepting the Freedom Charter, with its emphasis on multiracial objectives, had yielded to the influence of other racial groups like the Congress of Democrats and the Indian Congress. The clause declaring that South Africa belonged to 'all who live in it, black and white' aroused particular resentment. In the Africanist view, the only true 'owners' of South Africa were Africans. Others had merely 'stolen' the country. In 1959, the Africanists broke away to form their own group, the Pan-Africanist Congress (PAC).

From the outset, the PAC was badly organised and poorly led and it relied on little more than the notion that the time was ripe for action. Determined to establish its credentials as the leading nationalist group, it announced plans for a campaign of mass protest against the pass laws. It was at a PAC gathering in the township of Sharpeville on 21 March 1960 that police, facing a peaceful but restive crowd, in a moment of panic opened fire indiscriminately, killing 69 Africans, provoking worldwide condemnation of the South African government and a storm of African protest across the country. Two weeks later the ANC and the PAC were banned.

The sabotage campaign which Mandela initiated in 1961 was a forlorn enterprise from the start. The hope was that sabotage would scare off foreign investors, disrupt the economy and eventually cause white opinion to change. Mandela reasoned that providing there was no loss of life then race relations in the long term would not be impaired. But if black nationalist leaders failed to take decisive action, radical activists would resort to acts of terrorism which would have far more damaging consequences.

Abandoning his legal practice and forsaking all chance of a family life with his young wife, Winnie, and their two children, Mandela committed himself to working wholeheartedly as an underground leader. He became adept at travelling furtively around the country, assuming disguises, avoiding police traps and informers. Surreptitiously, he left South Africa in 1961 to organise facilities for guerrilla training and underwent a course of military training in Algeria, before returning in secret six months later. His skill in evading police capture, his daring in leaving the country, making contact with African leaders, then returning to pursue a clandestine existence, turned him into a legendary figure. In the press he became known as the 'Black Pimpernel' and as 'Verwoerd's most wanted man'. But 17 months after going underground, he was betrayed. Returning by car to Johannesburg from a trip to Natal in August 1962, he was stopped by police and arrested.

The sabotage campaign continued for 18 months. More than 200 attacks were made, mostly on public buildings, railway lines and power installations in major towns. Most of the sabotage attempts were clumsy and ineffectual. In terms of the objectives that Mandela had set, the campaign was a total failure. The impact on the economy was negligible. Foreign investors, far from being frightened away during the early 1960s, became more deeply involved. The white electorate, on the rare occasions when it was alerted to the danger of sabotage attacks, reacted in support of the government, not in opposition to it.

The government, meanwhile, adopted ever more repressive counter-measures, obliterating civil rights, on the grounds that it was dealing with a communist-inspired conspiracy to overthrow the state. Scores of men and women vanished into jails, to be subjected to solitary confinement, physical assaults and torture. With information obtained from detainees, police soon broke the back of underground resistance. In July 1963, they raided a farmhouse on a smallholding at Rivonia, north of Johannesburg, which Umkhonto used as its operational headquarters, capturing Sisulu and other key figures and acquiring an immense haul of incriminating documents. Joe Slovo, a key Umkhonto strategist, who escaped the dragnet, observed in retrospect how 'a mood of carelessness and bravado' had overtaken the conspirators. Few had been prepared to commit themselves to the rigours of real underground existence. Meanwhile, the site of the Rivonia headquarters had become known to so many activists that it represented a security weakness to the whole movement. 'Under torture,' wrote a former saboteur, Ben Turok, 'many victims found to their regret that they knew too much and that the police knew that they knew.' The end result for the black nationalist movement was disastrous. With its leaders imprisoned and its internal organisations destroyed, a silence descended for more than a decade. It was not broken until the 'children's uprising' of 1976.

In its quest for political rights from South Africa's white rulers, the ANC had tried polite deputations, public protests, petitions, civil disobedience, boycotts, sabotage, guerrilla warfare and urban insurrection. As it entered the 1990s, it had become more of a military organisation than a political one. Now, in 1994, it was to confront the white establishment at the polls.

The ANC's election manifesto bore little trace of this turbulent history. Like the Freedom Charter of 1955, it contained a large number of utopian notions. The list of promises was a long one. To overcome 'the social and economic devastation caused by generations of apartheid rule', the ANC undertook to launch what Mandela described as a 'gigantic' programme of public works, providing houses, essential services, electrification, better schools, roads, clinics and formal employment for millions of people. The specific targets laid out in the manifesto were ambitious: jobs and training for 2.5 million people over ten years; one million homes to be built over five years; electrification for 2.5 million rural and urban homes and running water and flush lavatories to over one million families over five years; ten years of free and compulsory education for all children; free school text books to be doubled in number within one year; affordable access to telecommunications; and basic health care for all South Africans. In addition, the small business sector would be developed by providing training and access to loans and by changing licensing laws. Land reform policies would assist farmers to gain access to credit, training and markets; and would guarantee restitution of land to victims of forced removals. Health care policies would pay special attention to children under five and to disease-prevention measures in poverty-stricken communities. Affirmative action programmes for Africans, Coloureds, Indians and other disadvantaged groups would focus on training and the upgrading of skills. The rights of women in land ownership, employment, taxation and in parliamentary representation would be vigorously promoted. On top of all this, the ANC promised to abolish value-added tax on basic foods and to reduce income tax for those earning less than R4,000 a month.

No explanation was forthcoming in the manifesto about how all these undertakings would be financed, other than a suggestion that the large sums already devoted to education, health and other government services could be more effectively spent by eliminating waste and corruption. The objectives were worthy enough in themselves, but amounted to little more than a wish-list.

A more detailed account of the ANC's policies was given in its 'Reconstruction and Development Programme' (RDP) upon which the election manifesto was based. The RDP endeavoured to provide a policy framework for a new administration. Its list of promises and moral imperatives was even longer than that contained in the manifesto and included everything from a 'living wage' for all workers to a national social security and pensions system, six months paid maternity leave, the redistribution of 30 per cent of agricultural land within five years and even a target reduction of ten per cent in traffic accidents. But once again, no costs were given; no suggestion of a funding strategy was made; no priorities were set; and policy options were left wide open.

The idea for a 'reconstruction' programme had been initiated in early 1993 by the trade union federation, Cosatu, with help from Communist Party leaders and some ANC officials, all concerned that the ANC might lose sight of its socialist principles once it was involved in a government of national unity. The co-ordinator was Cosatu's general secretary, Jay Naidoo, a talented organiser with a record of militant action, long regarded as a committed adversary of big business. Another influence was Joe Slovo, the SACP chairman, who had been involved in drawing up the Freedom Charter in 1955. Within the rank and file, there was a widespread conviction that only through socialism and central planning could promises of redistribution and reconstruction be achieved. The arrangement was that both trade union representatives and SACP members would stand for election on the ANC list, helping to bring in workers' votes for the ANC, and subsequently act as a caucus to advance socialist ideas within the new administration. The RDP went through six drafts before the final version was approved. Input came from a wide range of ANC-aligned organisations and forums, including the Macro Economic Research Group, a consortium of development economists and theoreticians from five South

African universities and from other campuses around the world.

The ANC itself had brought with it considerable ideological baggage from exile where for years it had stuck doggedly to the Freedom Charter promise to nationalise mines, banks and 'monopoly' industries. Mandela, upon his release from prison in 1990, had also endorsed the policy of nationalisation, much to the consternation of businessmen. Radical ideas and suggestions continued to surface in the following years, including proposals for government direction of private sector investment; political control of the Reserve Bank; state control of mineral marketing; and forced dismemberment of South Africa's powerful industrial conglomerates. There were also plans mooted for a wealth tax – essentially on white assets; a reconstruction levy; and minimum wage legislation. Behind much of the thinking lay not just faith in what state intervention could achieve but an assumption that an ANC-led government would have the capacity to undertake major economic and social engineering.

Tempered by the views of the local business community, foreign investors and international financial institutions like the World Bank and the International Monetary Fund, the RDP in its final version toned down the more coercive notions that were initially favoured. The ANC's interventionist instincts were, nevertheless, still recognisable. The RDP talked of increasing the public sector in 'strategic areas' through nationalisation, purchasing shareholdings in companies, and setting up new public corporations or joint ventures with the public sector. These policy options would be exercised depending on 'the balance of evidence'. State intervention was essential to redirect greater resources to social spending and black upliftment. Market forces alone would not rectify the legacy of apartheid. Indeed, the ANC continued to manifest strong distrust of markets and business in general. The word 'market' appeared in only eight of the RDP's 800 paragraphs, and in five of them it was to call for control of markets. It nevertheless recognised the importance of the role of the private sector and foreign investment and emphasised the need to develop a favourable investment climate. Reconstruction would not be feasible without the support of the private sector. Privatisation of parastatal corporations, as well as nationalisation, was mentioned as a policy option. Consideration would be given to reducing the public sector in certain areas. No mention was made in the RDP document of the word 'socialism'.

The ANC was anxious in particular to stress its commitment to fiscal and monetary discipline. The RDP upheld the independence of the Reserve Bank, though it proposed a change in the board of governors to include trade union representatives. Financing the programme would have to be done in ways that did not cause undue inflation or balance of payments difficulties. Most proposals could be financed by better use of existing resources rather than by borrowing or increased taxation. 'In the long run, the programme will redirect government spending, rather than increase it.' In the case of health care and education, the new targets could be achieved within the limits of existing fiscal arrangements. Development projects such as electrification could be largely self-financing. Although some new taxes would be imposed, on such areas as unutilised land, luxury goods and capital gains, the overall level of taxation would remain the same. Reforms of the tax system would enable more tax to be collected without having to raise taxation levels. In the case of middle-income earners, the tax burden needed to be reduced. The government deficit, meanwhile, would be kept within range of current levels of about six per cent, in line with a commitment the ANC had already given to the International Monetary Fund. No heavy foreign debts would be incurred. Foreign borrowing would be used ideally only to finance elements of the programme that could increase South Africa's capacity to earn foreign exchange. ANC economists emphasised how economic pragmatism had become the ANC's motto, spoke earnestly of the need 'to avoid the Latin American trap of macroeconomic populism' and pointed to those parts of the RDP document which urged private-sector involvement in economic policy-making. 'Key sectors of our society such as the business community must be consulted and encouraged to participate as fully as they may choose.'

Yet the threat of coercion still remained. One target was the financial sector. Financial institutions, said the RDP document, would be required to assist in the funding of individual programmes to meet basic needs, especially housing. These 'socially desirable' investments would be made without affecting risk profiles or decreasing returns on investment. If the banks failed to act voluntarily, they would be forced to follow government policy by law. 'If the major financial institutions do not take up socially desirable and economically targeted investments, the democratic government should consider some form of legislative compulsion such as prescribed assets' (the compulsory diversification of funds into government-determined investments). Measures would also be taken requiring banks to lend a rising share of their assets to small, black-owned enterprises and to make credit and other services available in low-income areas. The practice of 'red-lining' – imposing blanket bans on mortgage bonds to specific communities – would be outlawed and banks would be forced to provide reasons for turning down loan applications. Legislation would also be introduced to make the boards of mutual fund companies 'more socially responsible' and to ensure 'adequate representation' of trade unions on pension and provident funds. After an outcry from the business community following publication of these proposals in the sixth version of the RDP in January 1994, the ANC promised that consultation would be made with the financial sector before any changes in the regulatory environment were introduced.

Another target of the RDP, with potentially far more

serious consequences, was the mining sector. The mining industry provided the foundation of South Africa's modern economy. It was the country's largest exporter, its main foreign currency earner, the focus of international attention. What the ANC had to say about the mining industry had an impact far beyond the realms of the mining sector and far beyond South Africa's borders; it was taken as a reference point for ANC attitudes towards economic management as a whole.

The RDP, in its sixth version, claimed that the enormous wealth generated by the mining industry had been used 'for the benefit of the tiny white minority'. It was highly critical of the mining industry's performance. The value of various mineral exports, it said, could be massively increased by 'government intervention in output and pricing decisions' and by the 'use of a government minerals marketing auditor's office and a policy of national marketing of certain minerals'. It claimed that through these actions an estimated R3 billion a year could be raised in foreign exchange by 1997 for minerals other than gold and coal; an extra R1 billion could be earned through more and better-priced coal exports; and the export earnings of platinum-based metals could be increased by 40 per cent to R8 billion by the year 2007. No evidence was produced to support these claims.

The RDP also challenged the existing system of ownership of mineral rights. 'The minerals in the ground belong to all South Africans, including future generations. Thus we must seek the return of mineral rights to the democratic government, which should in turn give the people control over optimum exploitation of them.' State ownership of mineral rights would lead to an expansion of the mining industry by encouraging new entrants such as foreign mining companies and small mining enterprises. The principal objective was to transform the mining and mineral processing industry 'to serve all of our people, as a depleting resource that will eventually be exhausted'.

The reaction of the business community was that all

this sounded like a programme for the nationalisation of mineral rights and the establishment of a state-run marketing corporation with control over the pricing of mining output (in effect, a cartel arrangement). The mining industry's response was that continued private ownership of mineral rights was essential to ensure optimum exploitation of mineral resources and to maintain a stable environment that would encourage local and foreign investment. The mineral rights system, with its long-term security of tenure, had enabled mining companies to take a long view of exploration, market and technological development and of investment projects. It had been central to the development of the industry's leading-edge capabilities in deep-level, large and long-term mining projects and had encouraged massive expenditure by mining houses on exploration and the acquisition of rights; in the last decade alone, more than R6 billion had been spent. To transfer these rights to the government would be, in the words of the Chamber of Mines, 'complicated, costly and probably inequitable'. It would jeopardise long-term security of tenure, dent investor confidence and ultimately accelerate premature contraction of the industry. The people of South Africa already shared in the benefits of exploitation of mineral rights through taxation.

Moreover, there was no evidence that mining companies had failed to expand their production and exports where profitable opportunities existed, or to invest in beneficiation projects which were commercially attractive. The question of mining expansion had anyway to be seen in a wider context. In several commodities – platinum, manganese, vanadium and chrome – South Africa not only accounted for the major part of world production but also possessed reserves many times greater than annual world consumption. In these circumstances, expansion of South Africa's output could depress world prices to the detriment of existing producers and to economic prospects generally.

The mining industry was also scornful of any schemes for state control of mineral marketing or a cartel arrangement. A centralised marketing system would merely add to costs, reduce competitiveness and therefore market share, and promote inefficiency, again to the long-term detriment of export earnings and employment. Any suggestion that South Africa was operating a cartel would prompt customers to switch to alternative sources, and lead to a contraction of markets for South African commodities.

In general, the mining industry pronounced itself against any extension of government involvement. Mining was one of the world's riskiest businesses. Huge sums were at stake. The market for commodities was volatile and uncertain. If the government tried to alter by artificial means the risk and reward judgements made by private sector entrepreneurs, the result would be 'counter-productive'.

Faced with this barrage of criticism and a sudden loss of foreign confidence in South Africa's economic future, the ANC staged a retreat from its more controversial positions. The ANC did not intend, it said, to expropriate or nationalise mineral rights, nor to set up a state-run marketing system. Because of the complexity of the mineral rights issue, their transfer to the public domain would be a lengthy process, involving the use of such measures as incentives or taxes. Neither the profitability nor expansion of mining companies would be impaired. Moreover, any change in mineral rights policy, according to the RDP in its final version, would be done 'in full consultation with all stake-holders'. The ANC also dropped claims it had made about the sums that could be raised through government intervention. The RDP now read: 'Our principal objective is to transform mining and mineral-processing industries to serve all of our people. We can achieve this goal through a variety of government interventions, incentives and disincentives. Estimates suggest that the establishment of a government minerals marketing auditor's office and the national marketing of certain minerals would enable South Africa to realise greater foreign-exchange earnings. The management and marketing of our mineral exports must be examined together with employers, unions and the government to ensure maximum benefits for our country.'

As for the costs of the RDP, the ANC never produced any convincing sums. It remained 'a menu without prices'. In April, ANC officials came up with an overall figure of R39 billion to be spent over a period of five years and to be financed without any increase in government spending, taxation or fiscal deficit. But they but failed to provide an explanation for how this figure was arrived at. The National Party meanwhile commissioned a study of the costs of all the ANC's promises which claimed that in the first year alone they would amount to R70 billion and over five years to more than R600 billion, involving at least a doubling of taxation.

In constructing an economic strategy, the ANC had the difficult task of accommodating the views of both radical reformers and pragmatists and of reconciling the aspirations of its huge black constituency with the realities of South Africa's economic position and resources. The same constraints would affect an ANC-led government, though with even greater force. Yet the radical impulses of the ANC were certain to be kept alive by its two partners in the 'tripartite alliance', both guaranteed a prominent role in Mandela's administration: the South African Communist Party (SACP) and the Congress of South African Trade Unions (Cosatu).

The influence of members of the SACP was always far greater than the extent of its following. Driven underground in 1950, its members continued to provide a constant source of ideas which found their way into the ANC's political, economic and military strategy, both during the 1950s and later in exile. Through its links with the Soviet Union, the SACP was responsible for arranging much of the ANC's funding, training and weaponry. It played a key role in Umkhonto's intelligence operations and in military planning. Membership of the SACP provided a passport to the higher ranks of the ANC. It attracted a range of talented individuals, many of whom were regarded as 'the best and brightest' of those who went into exile.

The SACP was also slavishly pro-Soviet, Stalinist in outlook, faithfully following the Soviet model of socialism and praising Moscow's every move. Without Moscow's support, it would have been impotent. One of its most prominent members, Chris Hani, later reflected: 'Incorrectly, we went out of our way to justify everything the Soviet Union did. We thought it was our communist duty to defend and justify these positions because we were brought up in this tradition. We looked up to the Soviet Union as having solved most of the problems of building socialism.'

The collapse of Soviet communism deprived the SACP of both its socialist anchor and its main source of support. Seeking to explain what had gone wrong, the party's leading theoretician, Joe Slovo, argued in a discussion paper in 1989 that socialism itself was not at fault, merely the way in which it had been implemented. Democratic socialism in Eastern Europe had been abandoned in favour of one-party dictatorships. This had led to 'a political tyranny over the whole society'. The answer, therefore, was to pursue socialism within the framework of a multiparty democracy 'both in the democratic and socialist phases'. In the case of South Africa, it was of course not socialism which faced a crisis but capitalism. It was the capitalist system which had produced apartheid and which required overhauling.

Slovo's reasoning drew sharp criticism from some ANC quarters, notably from Pallo Jordan, an independent socialist. 'While Slovo recognises that the socialist countries degenerated into police states with their administrative and repressive organs possessed of inordinate powers, he never seems to broach the obvious questions: What gave rise to the need for such practices?' Jordan questioned whether the SACP had really rejected its Stalinist past as Slovo claimed. 'The political culture nurtured by the SACP's leadership over the years has resulted in a spirit of intolerance, petty intellectual thuggery and political dissembling among its membership.'

Not only was the SACP bereft of its Soviet moorings but it faced an entirely different political terrain in South Africa from the one for which it had planned for years. Instead of a revolutionary seizure of power, there came an era of negotiation, requiring compromises, concessions and attention to constitutional detail. SACP leaders, like Slovo and Hani, adapted well enough to the negotiation process. Indeed, it was Slovo's proposal for 'a sunset clause' providing for compulsory power-sharing that broke the deadlock in negotiations with the National Party at a critical juncture in 1992.

The difficulty for the SACP was that it was left with no clear role distinctive from that of the ANC. Several prominent figures allowed their membership to lapse, preferring to devote their allegiance solely to the ANC, now that it was on the threshold of power. No longer was the SACP the natural home of 'the best and the brightest'. Activists were left wondering what it was that they should do as party members that they could not do as ANC or trade union members and complained that the SACP had failed to forge an identity for itself as a working-class party with its own programme, practice and policy. Yet without its links to the ANC, the SACP would be destined for a life on the fringes of South African politics. The party's membership of 40,000 was too small for it to gain a political foothold of its own.

The role that the party saw for itself, therefore, was to act as the promoter of socialist objectives within the ANC. It was a role that the ANC was willing to facilitate, in recognition of the contribution that many

SACP members had made to the liberation struggle. In the ANC's national candidate list no less than 16 out of the first 50 candidates were SACP members; the figure was even higher if the number of lapsed communists on the list was included. But this effectively tied communists to the kind of compromises that the ANC would regard as necessary to establish a consensus in government policy, in much the same way as they had been obliged to accept the compromises contained in the Reconstruction and Development Programme. In place of revolutionary rhetoric, party members now talked of the need for 'well-planned quality interventions'.

Slovo accepted the need for the SACP to take 'a balanced approach'. He now rejected 'old style statism and commandist control', but pointed to the advantages which could be obtained from state intervention. Massive state intervention, he said, had laid the basis of the post-war economies of Japan, South Korea and Taiwan. 'But we do not advance a mechanical policy of across-the-board nationalisation. This would be extremely costly and would be met by an even greater flight of capital and skilled manpower. Compensation for nationalisation would tie up the budget and the balance of payments account for decades. It is impossible to satisfy popular economic aspirations in a declining economy.

'This should put paid to the continued projection of the SACP as heading the lobby within the ANC for the pursuit of nationalisation as a generalised formula for economic advance. The question which has to be answered is whether, in a specific area and in the concrete conditions, it will serve to strengthen the needs of economic growth and the capacity of the economy to meet the majority's needs.

'We have not abandoned our long-term aim of winning a future in which all the means of production are socialised to serve the interests of the whole of society. But that objective cannot be on the immediate agenda, and in the long term can be achieved only by ideological contest in a genuine multiparty democracy. In the meantime, reality dictates that for some time to come we need a mixed economy with a balanced role for both the private and public sectors.'

The trade union federation, Cosatu, was equally adamant about the need to strive for socialist objectives. It had already made significant inroads into policy-making through its involvement in initiating and developing the ANC's Reconstruction and Development Programme. It now envisaged a far more prominent role for unions not just in labour issues and through 'workplace empowerment' but in a wide range of public institutions and policy-making bodies.

With 15 affiliated unions, claiming a membership of 1.3 million, it represented a powerful workers' lobby. One of its largest affiliates, the National Union of Mineworkers, with 280,000 members, demanded both public ownership of the mining industry and 'the full participation' of the union in the running of the industry after the election. Cosatu in general wanted greater worker participation in decision-making at industry, company and plant level, as well as in government – 'real democratisation, not cosmetic,' said its general secretary, Sam Shilowa.

Union interests in the new parliament would be well represented. In return for union support in the election, union officials had been given 20 places on the ANC's candidates list. Several key trade union leaders had decided to opt for positions in government from which to further labour interests, the most prominent being Cosatu's outgoing general secretary, Jay Naidoo. 'I pledge to you we will not allow ourselves to be manipulated by any government,' declared Naidoo as he said farewell to Cosatu, shortly after his nomination for parliament had put him on the road to high government office.

Yet the dilemma for Cosatu concerning its future relationship with the ANC was far greater than it was for the SACP. The difficult choices facing union representatives inside government over the use of scarce resources were bound to conflict with the interests of unions outside. As the largest employer in the country, the government would have a particular interest in limiting public sector wage rises on the scale usually demanded by unions. The government would also have a keen interest, along with employers, in ensuring that South Africa's manufacturing industry achieved greater productivity and international competitiveness, another source of potential conflict with union interests if it meant retrenchment. For years to come, the big economic divide in South Africa would not be so much between white and black, but between the employed and the unemployed, a far larger constituency than the unions represented and one which an ANC government was pledged to do its utmost to defend. In those circumstances, wage increases which had an adverse impact on job creation would become a highly contentious issue.

Recognising the inevitability of such conflicts, some union leaders advocated a break in their close relationship with the ANC after the election. The idea of a workers' party was under constant discussion. The prospect for an ANC-led government in the post-apartheid era was that it was as likely to be in conflict with union objectives as in support of them.

National Party

Just as the ANC was proud to point to its record in fighting for political rights, so the National Party tried to distance itself from its own past. Yet the origins of the National Party lay in conditions of hardship and distress similar to those in which the ANC had been launched. Only two years separated their formation; the ANC was formed in 1912 in protest against the Union constitution which excluded African participation in government, and the National Party arose in 1914 in the cruel aftermath of the Anglo-Boer war. What occurred at that time was to have repercussions as far distant as the 1990s.

The Anglo-Boer war lasting from 1899 to 1902 had been fought by Britain to establish British supremacy throughout southern Africa, and by the Boers to preserve the independence of their republics. It left a legacy of bitterness among the Boers that endured for generations. Faced with guerrilla warfare for which they were ill-prepared, British military chiefs devised a scorched earth policy designed to erase all possible resistance by Boer commandos. Boer villages were razed to the ground; some 30,000 farmsteads were destroyed; cattle and sheep were slaughtered or carried away on such a scale that by the end of the war the Boers of the Orange Free State had lost half their herds, and those in the Transvaal three-quarters. To make sure that captured burghers would not fight again, the British deported thousands to prison camps in St Helena, Bermuda, Ceylon and India. Women and children were rounded up and placed in what the British called concentration camps where conditions were so appalling that some 26,000 died there from disease and malnutrition, most of them children under the age of 16.

After the Peace of Vereeniging, which formally marked the demise of the two Boer republics, the British authorities made every endeavour to re-establish Boer farmers on the land and to resuscitate the shattered economy of the new colonies. But their principal objective still remained, to establish British dominance in the region. English was made the official language, even though Boers outnumbered British. In the Transvaal and the Orange Free State the whole educational system was swept away. English teachers and English inspectors were appointed. English became the sole medium of instruction, except for a few hours a week allowed for teaching in Dutch. Immigration from Britain was encouraged in the hope that a permanent British majority among the whites in South Africa could be established.

Facing such a relentless onslaught from an imperial power at the peak of its fortunes, the Boer communities of South Africa seemed destined for decline and oblivion. The war had reduced them to an impoverished rural people. Many had been uprooted from the land altogether. Some 10,000 stayed on for months in concentration camps because they had nowhere else to go. The plight of the Boers was made even worse in 1903 by a record drought; that same year marked the beginning of an agricultural depression lasting six years. A growing number drifted to the towns hoping to find work, but the towns offered no refuge. They were the citadels of British commerce and culture where Boers from the *platteland*, possessing no skills or education, found themselves scorned and despised for their poverty, their country ways and their language.

A change of government in Britain in 1905 brought a more enlightened approach to its conquered territories. By 1907, the Transvaal and the Orange Free State were again self-governing under the control of the defeated Boer generals who had signed the terms of surrender. Hoping to arrange a more permanent settlement for the region, Britain then devised plans to include them in a white-ruled dominion, along with the Cape Colony and Natal.

The Union of South Africa was launched in 1910 with much goodwill and with the hope that the Boers and the British might now find a way of resolving their differences and merge into a single South African nation. The Prime Minister, Louis Botha, was a former Boer general well respected by both sides. His cabinet contained two other Boer generals, Jan Smuts and Barry Hertzog, as well as a large contingent of English-speaking South Africans. Dutch was recognised as an official language of the Union, equal to English. The 1910 election result showed that an overwhelming number of Afrikaners supported the government's policy of reconciliation. Outwardly there seemed a reasonable prospect that it could be achieved.

Yet fear and resentment of British domination ran deep. Many Afrikaners never accepted the idea of being part of the British Empire and mourned the loss of their own republics. Everywhere they were reminded of the presence of British authority. 'God Save the King' became the official anthem. The national flag was a British Red Ensign, with the Union coat of arms in a lower corner. The Privy Council in London, rather than the Supreme Court, was the final arbiter in the administration of justice. Moreover, on questions of war and peace, South Africa, under the 1910 constitution, was not a sovereign independent state, but bound by decisions of the British government. Most civil servants were English-speaking; even on the *platteland* English civil servants and teachers played a prominent role. The towns too were British. The British dominated industry, commerce and the mines and controlled the banks and finance houses. They also held an almost complete monopoly of industrial skills and training.

Believing that the sheer weight of British influence would eventually engulf the Afrikaner people and turn South Africa into a mere appendage of the British Empire, a group of Afrikaner leaders began openly to repudiate the policies of reconciliation which Botha and Smuts propounded. Among them was General Hertzog, the Minister of Justice, a former commando leader from the Orange Free State. Hertzog was at heart a republican. He had accepted the imperial connection only because it served to allay the fears of the English-speaking minority and thereby promote good relations between the two groups. But he was determined that South Africa should develop a separate and independent identity within the Empire, embracing both English and Afrikaners on a basis of complete equality.

Hertzog swiftly became the acknowledged champion of Afrikaner interests. His plan for a 'two-stream' policy for South Africa, by which Afrikaners and English would develop separately their own culture and traditions until the Afrikaner stream attained an equal status with the English, met with a ready response. Dropped from the cabinet in 1913, Hertzog travelled from village to village in the Orange Free State, promoting the Afrikaner cause and leaving in his wake a host of Afrikaner vigilance committees. The following year, with a handful of parliamentary colleagues, he formed the National Party. Its manifesto dwelt on three main points: South African interests first; mother-tongue education; and compulsory bilingualism in the public service.

South Africa's participation in the 1914 war outraged Hertzog's Nationalists and provoked serious conflict among Afrikaners. 'This is a war between England and Germany,' said Hertzog. 'It is not a South African war.' Several of his old Boer War colleagues thought the time was ripe for rebellion and issued a call to arms. In sporadic encounters lasting three months, government troops fought Afrikaner rebels.

The National Party benefited considerably from these events. In the 1915 general election, it made impressive gains, capturing nearly 30 per cent of the vote. In the 1924 general election, it won 33 per cent of the vote, obtaining more seats in the House of Assembly than any other party. By making a temporary alliance with the English-speaking Labour Party, Hertzog became the first Nationalist prime minister at the head of a coalition government.

Over the next eight years, Hertzog achieved many of the original goals of the National Party. In 1926 he obtained recognition from Britain of South Africa's claim to sovereign independence. He also settled the issue of a national flag which had stirred intense emotional debate. The language dispute was also resolved: in 1925, Afrikaans, the newly emerging language of Afrikaners, became an official language for the first time. Hertzog's outlook too began to change. He no longer feared that Afrikaner culture was in danger of being submerged by the weight of English tradition; there was no longer any reason, he said in 1930, why South Africans belonging to the two cultures should not feel and act together in the spirit of a consolidated South African nation.

But meanwhile the plight of much of the Afrikaner population had become ever more precarious; hundreds of thousands were facing destitution.

The 'poor white problem', as it was called, had cast a shadow over South Africa since the turn of the century. It grew out of the difficulties facing a rural people ill-prepared to cope with profound economic change. With the closing of South Africa's frontiers in the late nineteenth century, land was no longer readily available, but the white rural population continued to grow. As a people almost entirely tied to rural areas, the Boers were most directly affected. Their difficulties were made worse by poor farming methods, by drought and disease, and by inheritance laws which meant the continual subdivision of land into small, uneconomic holdings. The growth of commercial agriculture forced many *bywoners* – landless white tenants – off the land. Britain's policy during the Anglo-Boer War of laying waste vast areas of the Transvaal and the Orange Free State then compounded the process by destroying much that reconstruction could never replace.

The result was a steady exodus from rural areas to the towns – *die trek na die stad* – particularly to the goldfields of the Witwatersrand which by the turn of the century were producing one third of the world's gold supplies. In 1900 there were less than 10,000 Afrikaners living in towns; by 1904 the number had grown to 40,000 out of a total of 630,000 Afrikaners; by 1914 it amounted to nearly one third of the Afrikaner population. Yet as the Afrikaners found them, the towns were an alien and often hostile world. The language of industry, commerce and the civil service was overwhelmingly English; their own language, derided as a 'kitchen language', was treated with contempt. Lacking skills, education and capital, many were forced to seek work in competition with cheap black labour and to live cheek by jowl with blacks in slums on the ragged edges of towns. Urban poverty became as common as rural poverty.

In an attempt to deal with the problems of poor

white unemployment, Hertzog's coalition government, soon after it came to power in 1924, devised what was known as a 'civilised labour' policy, which meant in practice that wherever feasible whites replaced black workers in the public sector. This most affected the state-owned railways: between 1924 and 1933 the number of white employees increased by 13,000; some 15,000 Africans and Coloureds lost their jobs. Other government agencies and departments were similarly affected. The aim, said Hertzog, was to protect white living standards and to prevent the white man from becoming 'a white kaffir'.

Such measures, however, were not sufficient to keep pace with the flood of rural immigrants seeking work in towns. By 1926, the proportion of Afrikaners living in towns increased to 41 per cent. The number of poor whites also rose, from an estimated 106,000 in 1916 to 160,000 by 1923. Periodic droughts and depressions drove more and more whites off the land. In the depression years of 1928–32 the scale of misery affecting poor whites was immense. A Carnegie Commission report estimated that in 1930 about 300,000 whites, representing 17.5 per cent of white families, were 'very poor', so poor that they depended on charity for support, or subsisted in 'dire poverty' on farms. A further 31 per cent of whites were classified simply as 'poor', so poor they could not adequately feed and clothe their children. At least nine out of ten of these families were said to be Afrikaans-speaking. In rural areas, the Commission reported, many families were living in hovels woven from reeds or in mud huts with thatched roofs similar to those used by Africans. One third of these dwellings were said to be 'unsuitable for civilised life'. Many white families lived a narrow and backward existence. More than half of the children did not complete primary education. 'Education was largely looked upon, among the rural population, as something foreign, as a thing that had no bearing on their daily life and needs,' the Commission reported.

Facing social upheaval across the land and finding

themselves in the towns at the mercy of British commerce and culture, Afrikaners responded by establishing their own organisations to try to hold the *volk* together and preserve their own traditions. A host of welfare and cultural associations sprang up, including an organisation named the Afrikaner Broederbond. It began as a small select society, interested principally in the promotion of Afrikaner culture and language. But it was to grow into one of the most formidable organisations in South African history and to become a major factor in determining its fate.

For the first ten years of its existence, the Afrikaner Broederbond made little impact on Afrikaner society. Formed in 1918 in Johannesburg by a small band of ardent Afrikaners – railway clerks, policemen and clergymen – it set out to defend Afrikaner heritage at a time when, as one of its founders recalled, 'the Afrikaner soul was sounding the depths of the abyss of despair'. But it was frequently racked by internal dissension and purges.

Its prospects were transformed after Prime Minister Hertzog returned from the Imperial Conference in 1926 and announced that, as he considered the constitutional aims of the National Party had been largely satisfied by the Balfour Declaration granting South Africa dominion status, he would henceforth abandon republican demands. Outraged by this decision, hardcore nationalists within the Broederbond decided to expand their activities beyond the cultural field and infiltrate every facet of the Afrikaner community. From the late 1920s, the Broederbond developed into a tightly disciplined, highly secretive group which gradually extended its range and contacts throughout the country. Its aims were no longer confined merely to defending Afrikaner traditions. They were to establish Afrikaner domination. In a private circular issued in 1934, the chairman of the Broederbond, Professor van Rooy, wrote: 'Let us keep constantly in view the fact that our chief concern is whether Afrikanerdom will reach its eventual goal of mastery [*baasskap*] in South

Africa. Brothers, our solution for South Africa's troubles is ... that the Afrikaner Broederbond shall rule South Africa.'

A fundamental rupture in Afrikaner politics occurred in the 1930s. As South Africa struggled to cope with the effects of the great depression, Hertzog agreed to form first a coalition with General Smuts's opposition South Africa Party and then to merge their two parties as the United Party. Hertzog's purpose, now that he no longer feared the threat of British imperialism, was to establish *Suid Afrikaanse volkseenheid* – a unity between all South Africa's whites. But to Afrikaner nationalists, this threatened both their republican aspirations and their hopes for eventual Afrikaner control. Instead of Hertzog's *Suid Afrikaanse volkseenheid*, they wanted *Afrikaner volkseenheid*.

The nationalist mantle now passed to Dr Daniel Malan, a former Dutch Reformed Church *predikant*, who had forsaken the pulpit for politics, becoming leader of the National Party in Cape Province. Malan represented a new breed of political intellectual emerging from the ranks of urban middle-class Afrikaners and destined to play a decisive role in the development of Afrikaner nationalism. Repudiating Hertzog's 'betrayal', he launched the Gesuiwerde National Party (GNP) – a 'purified' National Party claiming to stand for the aims and objectives of 'true' Afrikaners. *Gesuiwerde* nationalism differed markedly from any of its predecessors. It was not simply a return to the 'pure' nationalism of the past, of the kind once espoused by Hertzog. It was a new nationalism brought forth from the depths of deprivation, hardened by new ideology and driven by a ruthless determination to dominate.

The GNP made little impact when it was launched in 1933. The mood of the country's white population was clearly in favour of coalition. When the split occurred, only 18 members of parliament (out of 150) followed Malan into the GNP. For the next few years Malan's nationalists remained in the wilderness. Hertzog dismissed them as a group of fanatics merely intent on stirring up discord and hatred. Yet during that time the foundations were laid for a dramatic revival of nationalist fortunes.

At the centre of this revival, directing events behind its screen of secrecy, lay the Broederbond. By the mid-1930s its influence extended to every level of Afrikaner society and to every area of the country. Its élite membership, carefully selected and bound together by oath, had risen to 1,400 in 80 separate cells, mostly professional men, teachers, academics, clergymen and civil servants. Through front organisations, the Broederbond possessed a tight grip over Afrikaner cultural activities. It had penetrated the civil service and the teaching profession, and its efforts were now directed to infiltrating members into key positions in all leading institutions. With the formation of the GNP, it had also gained what was effectively a political wing. Malan and other nationalist MPs were swiftly recruited to its ranks.

It was also under the Broederbond's auspices that a coherent ideology for the new nationalism began to take shape. At Afrikaans universities like Potchefstroom, Pretoria and Stellenbosch and at favourite meeting places like the Koffiehuis in Cape Town, nationalist intellectuals gathered for intense and often abstruse discussion on the finer points of nationalist doctrine. Their theories were aired in obscure journals and pamphlets, often provoking fierce dispute. New ideas were imported by young Afrikaners returning to South Africa from study in Europe, where they had been strongly influenced by the rise of European fascism. The audience that this intellectual ferment reached was limited. The vast majority of Afrikaners showed no interest either in nationalist theory or in the people promoting it. Yet, through their discussions, the intellectuals accomplished a transformation of Afrikaner nationalism and eventually succeeded in gaining a mass following for it by embellishing Afrikaner history with powerful myths that endured for generations.

The new nationalism – Christian-Nationalism, as it was called – was essentially a blend of the Old Testament and modern politics. At its core was the notion that the Afrikaners were members of an exclusive *volk* created by the hand of God to fulfil a special mission in South Africa. Their history, their language, their culture, being divinely ordained, were unique. They were an organic unity from which 'foreign elements', such as English-speakers, were excluded. This vision of the Afrikaners as a chosen people, based on Calvinist ideas, had first been expounded systematically by Paul Kruger, President of the South African Republic (the Transvaal) from 1881 to the British conquest in 1902, and a firm believer in the scriptures of the Old Testament. Now it became an integral part of nationalist mythology. As Professor van Rooy, chairman of the Broederbond, explained in 1944: 'In every People in the world is embodied a Divine idea and the task of each People is to build upon that idea and to perfect it. So God created the Afrikaner People with a unique language, a unique philosophy of life, and their own history and tradition in order that they might fulfil a particular calling and destiny here in the southern corner of Africa.'

Another integral part of the new nationalism was the emphasis placed on past triumphs and sufferings of the Afrikaner people. Their history was portrayed as an epic struggle against two powerful enemies, the British and the blacks, both intent of their annihilation and only prevented from succeeding by divine intervention. 'The last hundred years', Malan asserted, 'have witnessed a miracle behind which must lie a divine plan.' In the context of the 1930s, the greatest threat to Afrikanerdom was seen to come not from the blacks, as it was at a later stage, but from British imperialism and its allies in the English-speaking population. Every effort was made to explain the present plight of the Afrikaner people by attributing it to the evil designs of British policy. One episode after another from the past was cited as evidence of British oppression, starting from the moment the British took possession of the Cape in 1806 and imposed their rule over its Boer inhabitants.

The exodus the Boers had begun from the Cape in the 1830s became known as 'the Great Trek', a defiant gesture against imperial Britain on behalf of the Boer nation. And the Great Trek itself became evidence that God had summoned the Boers to the same mission as the Israelites of the Old Testament who had trekked from Egypt to escape the Pharaoh's yoke and to establish a promised land. Celebrations of the centenary of the Great Trek of the *voortrekkers* in 1938 generated a torrent of nationalist emotions.

The same heroic myths were woven about the Afrikaners in their conflicts with the African population. At the battle of Blood River in 1838, a Boer commando, totalling 468 men, together with Coloured and African servants and about 60 African auxiliaries, formed their wagons into a defensive circle – a *laager* – and repulsed a Zulu army, perhaps 10,000 strong. The Zulus retreated leaving about 3,000 dead; the commando lost not a single member. The occasion was held to be of the utmost significance to the Afrikaner people, not just because it marked a famous military victory but because the events of that time were taken as proof that God had selected the Afrikaners as His Chosen People. What was especially important was a pledge, said to have been made by members of the commando a few days before the battle occurred, that if God granted them a victory, they would build a memorial church in His honour and commemorate the anniversary as a day of thanksgiving for ever more. Thus the victory at Blood River, following the covenant that had been made, and won in the face of overwhelming numbers, was held to be a sign of God's commitment to the Afrikaner people. Like the stories subsequently told about the Great Trek, the covenant made at Blood River came to mean far more to later generations than to the participants themselves.

This version of Afrikaner history was fortified by the work of popular Afrikaans writers like Totius, Langenhoven and Malherbe who dwelt on the heroic deeds of nineteenth-century figures and linked them to the present struggles of the Afrikaner people. The idea was to establish a mythical unity binding the Boer people together through their trials and torments. In a time of great social upheaval, when *platteland* communities were disintegrating and simple rural people were being flung headlong into the maelstrom of industrial society, when old values and traditions were being destroyed and 'foreign' interests prevailed, the need for unity – *volkseenheid* – was seen to be paramount. Through unity, the Afrikaner *volk* could overcome all the oppression and exploitation that imperialism had inflicted upon them.

The Afrikaner intellectuals who developed this nationalist doctrine were not only concerned with theory. Appalled by the poverty and degradation they witnessed among Afrikaners, they sought practical ways to improve the poor whites' lot. The solution, they believed, lay in developing Afrikaner economic strength to counter the weight of 'foreign' banks, mining houses and trading interests. In answer to 'Anglo-Jewish' capitalism, they proposed *'volkskapitalisme'*. The basis for their economic recovery was to be the savings of Afrikaner workers and farmers and self-help schemes – *helpmekaar*. In much the same way as the network of Afrikaner cultural institutions had succeeded in promoting Afrikaner culture, now a network of Afrikaner business interests would be used to break through to the economic heights.

In post-war years, as concern about white poverty receded, Malan's National Party turned its attention increasingly to the 'black peril' – *swart gevaar* – issue. Not only were there signs of growing truculence among the black population, but whites were reminded anew of the numbers that threatened to swamp them. The 1946 census figures showed that whites were a declining proportion of the population. Since 1910 the white population had increased by little more than a million to 2.4 million, whereas the non-white population, as it was called, had expanded from 4.5 million to 9 million. About 60 per cent of Africans were now living in white-designated areas, while only 40 per cent were based in Reserves.

The solution proposed by the National Party was the policy of apartheid. Developed by Afrikaner intellectuals in the 1940s and given the blessing of the Dutch Reformed Churches, it involved racial separation in as many spheres as possible. All this, affirmed the churches, was in accordance with Christian doctrine: God had ordained the division of nations and wished them to be kept separate. Texts from the Bible were cited as proof.

In the election campaign of 1948, the National Party used every opportunity to play on the electorate's racial anxieties. The choice for whites, the Nationalists said, was between 'integration and national suicide' on the one hand or 'apartheid' and protection of a 'pure white race' on the other. They paid particular attention to the interests of working-class Afrikaners facing competition from cheap African labour. By 1948, about half of the white Afrikaans-speaking population lived in urban areas. A large proportion were miners, railwaymen, transport, factory and steel workers for whom the Nationalist slogan of apartheid, promising protection of jobs, had a potent appeal. The Nationalist programme also attracted Afrikaner farmers who wanted tighter controls imposed on African movement to overcome acute shortages of African labour. Throughout the campaign, Malan harped on the need for unity among Afrikaners. In total, they constituted about 60 per cent of the white population. 'Bring together all who, from inner conviction, belong together' was his constant rallying cry.

The 1948 election transformed the face of South Africa. Malan's government was the first in the history of the Union to consist exclusively of Afrikaners; all but two ministers were members of the Broederbond. The new cabinet used its powers of patronage on a scale hitherto unknown in South Africa. The upper echelons of the civil service, the armed forces, the police and parastatal organisations like the railways were purged of English-speakers and filled with carefully selected Afrikaners, usually members of the Broederbond. The state sector became virtually an Afrikaner preserve. The legal profession eventually faced the same treatment; senior English-speaking members of the bar were systematically overlooked in the appointment of judges. The government also favoured Afrikaner business interests. Government accounts were switched to Afrikaner financial institutions; government contracts were awarded to Afrikaner companies; parastatal development organisations were used to promote Afrikaner participation in industry. The public sector was greatly expanded, doubling its share of fixed investment over the next 25 years, giving the Afrikaner establishment greater control over the economy and the means to promote Afrikaner business interests. The range of state enterprises extended from railways and harbours to iron and steel production, electric power generation, heavy engineering and oil production from coal. At a senior level these enterprises were manned almost exclusively by Afrikaners and used as training fields for Afrikaner scientists and business leaders. Out on the *platteland*, Afrikaner farmers were assisted at every turn by favourable prices fixed by state marketing boards, by government subsidies, tariffs, huge research funds, modernisation programmes and official controls to ensure a regular supply of cheap black labour. One Afrikaner historian commented that South African agriculture had many of the characteristics of a gigantic system of outdoor relief. The Afrikaner working class also prospered. Almost every skilled trade and craft was reserved for white workers, together with an increasing range of low-skilled jobs – traffic policemen in Cape Town, passenger-lift operators in Johannesburg, production jobs in the clothing, building, metallurgical and mining industries. Government employment was also used to shelter a growing number of whites. By 1968, one in five economically active whites was employed in official agencies at central, provincial and local levels. An Afrikaner economist once described all this as nothing better than 'legalised group plundering'. In modern parlance, it could be described as affirmative action with a vengeance.

In dealing with the African population, the National Party was far more ruthless. Malan, in his mid-seventies when he came to office, possessed no grand design for the African population; this was left to later generations of leaders. But he initiated what was to become a vast apparatus of laws, regulations and bureaucracies enforcing racial separation. Population registers were drawn up allocating every person to a particular racial group; mixed marriages and inter-racial sex were banned; separate residential areas were established; African 'black spots' – freehold areas lying within white urban districts – were wiped out; separate facilities were established in all spheres of public life – separate buses, trains, post offices, stations, restaurants, theatres, park benches, elevators, libraries, liquor stores and taxis. Coloureds were stripped of the vote – a right to which they had been entitled for 100 years.

Then came grand apartheid. Its architect, Hendrik Verwoerd, was not a true Afrikaner. He had been born in a small village near Amsterdam, Holland, in 1901 to Dutch parents who emigrated to South Africa when he was two years old. His family thus bore none of the scars of the Anglo-Boer War which afflicted so much of the Afrikaner population. For Verwoerd, there were no tales of family heroism, no link to the *voortrekkers* of the past, no personal sense of anguish at the fate of a defeated people. In view of the importance that Afrikaner nationalists attached to their own history, it was a considerable irony that the most powerful leader they were ever to find had no place in it. But Verwoerd believed no less firmly than other Afrikaner leaders that not only were his policies the result of divine intervention but that his own rise to prominence had been as well. 'I do not have the nagging doubt of ever wondering whether perhaps I am wrong,' he declared.

The social system that Verwoerd proceeded to construct brought hardship and misery to much of the African population. His ultimate objective, as he explained it, was total territorial separation between white and black. To that end, the African population was divided into different tribal groups and assigned to separate homelands. No previous attempt had ever been made to implement territorial segregation on this tribal basis. Hitherto the whole emphasis of government policy had been simply to segregate black from white. Now Verwoerd decreed that the African people were not homogeneous, but a collection of separate national groups divided by language and culture. Their roots lay in separate homelands; there they would be accorded 'separate freedoms'. This principle would apply not only to rural blacks but to urban blacks, regardless of how many generations they had lived in towns; they were all deemed to be citizens of the new homelands. By emphasising tribal loyalties, Verwoerd intended to keep the black population divided. Division of the blacks became a central part of his strategy. It was division of the blacks that would counter the challenge mounted by African nationalists, destroy the notion of black majority rule and guarantee supremacy of the whites for all time.

To satisfy Verwoerd's new vision for South Africa, more than three million people were uprooted in 'forced removals'. Already overcrowded and impoverished, homelands had to cope with an endless flow of displaced Africans – tenants, 'squatters', redundant farm labourers, urban dwellers, farmers driven out of rural 'black spots' – 'superfluous' people, as they were called. During the 1960s, the homelands' population nearly doubled. For the vast majority there, the only means of survival was the migrant labour system, which is what the government intended. In 1970, it was estimated that more than two million men spent their lives circulating as migrants between their homes and urban employment. Many were deprived of all normal family and social life, confined for months on end to a bleak and barren existence in overcrowded barracks which were notorious for high rates of drunkenness and violence. Others spent hours each day travelling long distances to work in packed buses and trains, rising before dawn and returning home late into the night.

In urban areas, meanwhile, black townships were kept as unattractive as possible to discourage any idea of permanent black urbanisation. Few urban amenities were ever provided; black urban businessmen were prevented by government restrictions from expanding their enterprises. In the sprawling city of Soweto, outside Johannesburg, in the 1960s, only a fraction of houses had electricity or adequate plumbing. Few paved roads were built. There were no modern shopping centres or office blocks, not a single pharmacy or bakery. From the mid-1960s, construction of family housing in urban areas virtually came to a halt. Priority was given instead to building hostels for migrant labour. Slum conditions were common. By 1970 in Soweto an average of 13 people lived in each house or 'matchbox', as they were called. To enforce control over African movement, an ever more repressive system of influx controls and pass laws was imposed.

White critics of the apartheid system were dismissed with contempt either as being ill-informed or ill-intentioned, possibly communist sympathisers. The liberal press, which exposed some of the worst excesses of the system, was constantly harassed. Dissent of any kind invited the attention of the security police. An equally tight grip was kept over literature and entertainment. The state-controlled radio network, meanwhile, packed with members of the Broederbond, poured out an endless stream of propaganda, dwelling on how apartheid, in Verwoerd's words, had brought 'happiness, security and stability' and contrasting it with the miseries of life in black-ruled states in Africa. National Party rule reduced white society to an insular and inbred world which demanded conformity. 'Opposing apartheid,' observed a prominent Afrikaner critic, 'is worse than murder to some Afrikaners. You endanger the nation by refusing to conform.'

The apartheid machine reached its zenith in the 1970s. Through the use of harsh and arbitrary measures, the government succeeded in reducing the rate of African urbanisation. But it still failed to halt the increase. Between 1960 and 1970 the number of Africans living legally in towns rose from 3.5 million to 5.1 million, nearly two million more than the number of urban whites. Moreover, the system was soon at loggerheads with the demands of South Africa's growing economy. Shortages of skilled labour were hampering economic growth. The reservoir of white skills had simply run out. White businessmen, for reasons of self-interest, argued that the only solution was to scrap the job reservation system giving whites a monopoly of skilled work and to allow blacks to move upwards in the labour market. This involved better education and training facilities for blacks, higher pay and a more secure urban environment. Step by step, the apartheid system was forced by economic reality to retreat. Social apartheid, too, began to fray at the edges. Botha, in the early years of his administration in the 1980s, conceded trade union rights for black workers and permanent residence rights for blacks in urban areas; then, in response to the townships revolt in the mid-1980s, he accepted the inevitability of black urbanisation, scrapping influx controls and pass laws which had burdened the African population for much of the twentieth century. A hard core of Afrikaners held fast to the idea that the apartheid system of old could still be preserved and broke away to form the Conservative Party. But by the 1980s, not even the Dutch Reformed Churches argued any more that it was all in accordance with Christian teaching.

The legacy of the National Party, after nearly half a century in power, was a country riven by political and racial animosity, with massive inequalities in education, housing and health, overcrowded and bankrupt homelands, economic decline and a culture of violence that would take years to root out.

It was against this background that F. W. de Klerk presented his credentials for re-election. The National Party did its best to draw attention away from its record by claiming credit for the changes that had occurred in South Africa. But the result was to leave the National Party fighting on terrain on which the ANC already had a superior claim while offering no clear view of the future. 'We swept away the apartheid laws. We unbanned the ANC and others. We steered our country in a new direction,' asserted de Klerk in an election advertisement. 'Soon we will have a new constitution, protecting the rights of all South Africans and giving everyone the right to vote. Our economy is improving. We are selling our products across the world. Investments are starting to flow into our country, creating new jobs and prosperity. We are competing on the sports fields of the world. All this happened because the National Party made it happen.'

In its election manifesto, the National Party took the same line, extolling the reforms initiated by de Klerk who, it said, had 'ended apartheid, released political opponents and made this election possible'. De Klerk, it claimed, was 'recognised throughout the world as the man who really liberated South Africa'. In sanctimonious tones, it asserted that it was the National Party which, in negotiations, had safeguarded democracy, secured a charter on fundamental rights and limited the power of government by ensuring a federal outcome. 'Freedom is worth nothing if it can be taken away at the whim of the government.' Coming from a party which had just spent 40 years in government obliterating basic human rights, this was a less than convincing position.

The manifesto was written in simplistic language. Its section on 'peace and prosperity' – one of the party's main slogans – read: 'There can be peace only if all people enjoy prosperity. Only if your neighbour has enough to eat can you sleep peacefully ... A person without a job cannot be a happy person ... A family without a house cannot be a happy family ... A young person without proper education cannot be very satisfied ... A community without proper health care cannot be prosperous.'

No detail was given about the National Party's policies. The manifesto merely praised the government's past economic performance and made a series of pledges about 'sound' economic management. This involved a market-based economy; taxation that promoted savings, investment and initiative; a favourable investment climate that created employment; deregulation; effective competition; and sound monetary policies secured by a high degree of autonomy for the Reserve Bank. Some form of state intervention was needed to direct greater resources to social spending and to the improvement of black education, training, health and housing. But, said the manifesto, 'socialism and communism destroy the economy – this has been proved over and over in the formerly socialist countries of Eastern Europe and in those African countries which tried it.' Only private enterprise and a market-based economy could create prosperity.

The National Party manifesto, with its limited vision of the future, was designed not so much to capture a mass market as to attract those worried or concerned about the more radical noises coming from the ANC. In essence, however, there existed a considerable measure of convergence in the objectives of each party. Both were strong on the virtues of motherhood and apple pie.

Pan-Africanist Congress of Azania

In breaking away from the African National Congress in 1959, the PAC promoted two potent ideas: 'African' rule of South Africa, and the return of the land to indigenous black people. Explaining the party's policy at its inaugural conference, the PAC's president, Robert Sobukwe, a 35-year-old lecturer in African languages at the University of Witwatersrand, declared: 'We aim, politically, at government of the Africans, by Africans, for Africans, with everybody who owes his only loyalty to Africa and who is prepared to accept the democratic rule of an African majority, being regarded as an African. We guarantee no minority rights because we think in terms of individuals not groups.'

Since the flurry of activity in the year before it was banned, the PAC had achieved little of significance. Subjected to mass raids and arrests in 1960, it became virtually leaderless. In 1961, it launched an underground armed wing with aims that included the murder of whites. Given the name 'Poqo', a Xhosa expression meaning 'alone' or 'pure' to emphasise its African origins, it was poorly organised but inspired a large following, notably in the Western Cape, with visions of an imminent black uprising. A leaflet left in a black township outside Cape Town in December 1961 declared: 'We are starting again Africans ... we die once. Africa will be free on 1 January. The white people shall suffer, the black people will rule. Freedom comes after bloodshed. Poqo has started.' In random, haphazard operations, Poqo supporters were responsible for the killing of African policemen and informers, for a brief uprising in Paarl in 1962, and for the murder of five whites in a road-builders' camp in Transkei.

In 1963, plans for a more general uprising were prepared by a group of PAC leaders in exile in Maseru, the capital of Lesotho. Instructions were sent to Poqo supporters to manufacture their own weapons with whatever materials were to hand and to collect food and clothing. On a given date, they were to launch simultaneous attacks on strategic points such as police stations and power installations before turning their attention to massacring whites indiscriminately. The plan began to go wrong when Potlake Leballo, a wayward but ambitious figure who had inherited the PAC's leadership from Sobukwe, gave warning of the uprising two weeks before it was due to start, at a press conference in Maseru, claiming that 100,000 armed followers were waiting for his signal, thereby enabling South African police to take pre-emptive action.

Poqo's activities in the early 1960s represented the peak of the PAC's efforts in three decades of 'armed struggle'. In exile, it became renowned for internal disputes and squabbles, and its armed wing, renamed the Azanian People's Liberation Army (Apla), was noticeably inactive.

It was only after de Klerk lifted the ban on the PAC in 1990 and permitted free political activity that Apla gained notoriety for its armed attacks. The PAC had considerable difficulty in coming to terms with the idea of a negotiated settlement in South Africa and clung tenaciously to the rhetoric of armed struggle. 'One settler, one bullet' became a popular slogan in the 1990s. The year 1993 was termed the 'Year of the Great Storm' in which Apla would step up the armed struggle; the year 1994 was given the title 'The Year of the Bullet and Ballot'.

In deciding whether to join the negotiations at Codesa, the PAC split: senior leaders wanted to participate but a large number of branches accused them of selling out and declared their autonomy. At a special congress in December 1991, a majority voted to boycott Codesa. By the time multiparty talks resumed in 1993, the PAC was ready to join in, but continued as well to support the notion of armed struggle. Apla's sporadic attacks on white farmers and other white targets were carried out with the full approval of senior PAC officials. Apla, said the PAC's national organiser, Maxwell Nemadzivhanani, was not fighting for power-sharing but to 'get the land back from the settlers'. White farmers would always be a target. 'The more you kill them, the more you come closer to liberation.'

At its annual conference in Transkei in December 1993,

the PAC agreed to participate in the election, but as a sop to radical factions, such as the self-styled Revolutionary Watchdogs, which opposed participation, it stressed once more its commitment to armed struggle. Two weeks later, in what appeared to be a repeat performance of a previous suspected Apla attack, gunmen burst into a tavern in Cape Town, killing four people and wounding six others. The outrage this attack caused, coming at a time when other parties were preparing their election campaigns, led Tanzania, which had provided a headquarters for the PAC since the 1960s, to end its support for the group and eventually forced the PAC's leadership to announce it was suspending armed struggle. This decision in turn was condemned as 'capitulation' by party radicals determined to continue with armed struggle until 'majority rule' was achieved.

The PAC thus entered the election in serious disarray. Both its student wing, the Pan-Africanist Students' Organisation (Paso) and its youth wing, the Azanian National Unity, together with other radical factions, were opposed to elections.

Its message to the electorate was simple: all land would be appropriated by the state and redistributed to 'Africans'. No protection of freehold title would be given; no monetary compensation would be made; and no subsequent land transactions would be allowed. Every homeless person would be guaranteed a plot of land. 'We promise you the return of the land of our forefathers which was taken from you by force,' said the PAC's president, Clarence Makwetu, a Transkei farmer. 'If it means we must go back to the bush to return our land, we will do so.'

The PAC also favoured changing the name of South Africa to Azania. It was a name derived from an Arabic description for East Africa which early Greek cartographers had put on their maps of the world and which the writer Evelyn Waugh had later used for an African kingdom in his novel *Black Mischief*.

Apart from the issue of land redistribution, the PAC put forward no coherent policies. It also possessed no organisational ability and minimal funds. The version of Africanism which many of its officials now expounded had become no more than a thinly disguised form of racism, a travesty of what the founding father of Africanism, Anton Lembede, had envisaged in the 1940s. Yet the PAC's slogans on land and its anti-white rhetoric had a popular appeal. And it was on this that the PAC staked everything.

Inkatha Freedom Party

Since its formation in 1975, Inkatha had been controlled with single-minded determination by Chief Mangosuthu Buthelezi. Using his connections with the Zulu royal family and his position as Chief Minister of the KwaZulu homeland, he built Inkatha into the largest black political organisation in South Africa in the years that the African National Congress was banned.

Initially, the ANC, in exile, supported Inkatha, believing that it would help to undermine the apartheid system. But a feud soon developed between the two which was eventually to lead to ten years of civil strife in KwaZulu/Natal and on the Witwatersrand, and which continued for most of the election campaign.

Buthelezi's ambition was to build up Zulu nationalism and to use it as a base from which to campaign for a federal system in South Africa, thus giving KwaZulu/Natal, with himself in command, a large measure of autonomy. He opposed sanctions against South Africa, supported market economics, condemned the use of violence and collaborated with the Pretoria authorities in attempting to contain the ANC – all of which gained him the admiration and support of many whites, especially in Natal.

Buthelezi was consistent in advocating a federal solution for South Africa, but his tactics of boycott, bluster and threat during the course of constitutional negotiations, instead of attempting to build a tactical alliance with other federally-minded parties, effectively undermined what prospects there were of securing one. He preferred to listen to the advice of hardline whites like Walter Felgate rather than to more respected members of his retinue, and sought a dubious alliance with white extremists and homeland dictators in trying to block the negotiations' progress.

His power base amongst the Zulu people meanwhile steadily eroded as the community divided into rival camps supporting Inkatha or the ANC, or merely tried to steer clear of their increasingly violent conflict. By invoking the king's support and projecting Inkatha as the defender of the Zulu monarchy, Buthelezi played his master card. However, he then came to depend on Zwelethini's determination to stand by him, in the face of offers from Mandela and de Klerk that secured for the monarchy a role in the future with even greater prestige than he had obtained under Buthelezi. If Buthelezi had joined the electoral process in February 1994, having forced significant concessions from Mandela, he could have claimed a significant political victory. By overplaying his hand, he threw away all tactical advantage, lost further support and left himself with less than a week in which to canvass.

In the deserted cabinet room in the KwaZulu Legislative Assembly, Buthelezi laughed as he told a reporter, 'I don't think any politician in the world would agree to fight an election in only seven days. I must be the most insane politician.'

Democratic Party

For more than 30 years, the Democratic Party and its previous incarnations such as the Progressive Party represented the voice of liberal conscience in South Africa. Their stand against the onslaught of apartheid was often a lonely one. In the 1960s, a solitary member of parliament, Helen Suzman, waged a parliamentary struggle single-handed, despised by the National Party and ostracised by the white opposition United Party. During the 1970s and 1980s, the white liberal vote increased; in the 1989 election, it represented 20 per cent of the white electorate. But in the wake of National Party reforms, support for the liberal cause, according to opinion polls, appeared largely to evaporate. As the Democratic Party ruefully acknowledged, the National Party had finally done what liberals had been urging it to do for years.

In the 1994 election, the Democratic Party presented itself as the guardian of human rights and civil liberties, capable of protecting people from the abuse of power and totalitarian tendencies of both the ANC and the National Party, and offering 'clean hands', free of both corruption and violence. The programme it proposed included: tight control of government expenditure; balanced budgets; lower taxation; privatisation of state assets; the phasing out of exchange controls; massive labour-intensive housing and development programmes in partnership with the private sector; an improved network of primary health facilities; and at least ten years free and compulsory education.

The difficulty the Democratic Party faced was in finding a black as well as a white audience for this programme. Its leadership was capable and energetic, but largely white. In the black community, the Democratic Party was little known and barely understood.

Freedom Front

The Freedom Front was launched in quest of an ideal which seemed unattainable. For its founder, General Constand Viljoen, achieving an Afrikaner *volkstaat* was 'an all-consuming obsession'. Unlike his former colleagues on the far right of Afrikaner politics, he could see no merit in trying to obtain a *volkstaat* through military action and broke with them in March 1994, registering the Freedom Front for participation in the election with only minutes to spare before the deadline. Yet whatever dedication and resolve Viljoen brought to bear, the ideal was likely to remain beyond his reach.

His first task, as agreed with the African National Congress, was to gain a sufficient share of the Afrikaner vote to prove that he had the necessary level of support for the idea of a *volkstaat* to be pursued further through the mechanism of a Volkstaat Council. The election results would indicate which areas might form the basis of a *volkstaat*.

Viljoen's concept of a *volkstaat* was a territory that would maintain constitutional and economic links to the rest of South Africa but allow Afrikaners to achieve 'self-determination' and gain a majority there without infringing on the rights of others living in the area. Since there was not a single magisterial district in South Africa with a white majority, let alone an Afrikaner majority, the practical side of Viljoen's plans remained obscure.

However unrealistic his plans seemed, Viljoen himself was accorded high respect by negotiators in both the ANC and the government. A former defence force chief who retired in 1985 to farm in the Eastern Transvaal, he was drawn into active politics by colleagues who asked him to provide strategic leadership to the squabbling factions of the far right. While other Volksfront leaders favoured military action, Viljoen, with far greater war experience than any of them, persisted in confidential negotiations with the ANC and the government. His decision to register the Freedom Front for the election, giving right-wing Afrikaners a political outlet, helped defuse what otherwise could have turned into a serious right-wing threat to the election process.

Mandela, in an interview shortly before the election, paid his own tribute: 'General Viljoen is a very honest man, and I would welcome him in a Government of National Unity. It would strengthen the government. He may not be so astute politically – he is a soldier – but he is a man of integrity and in all the meetings I have had with him I have come out feeling that this is a man with whom we can work and solve problems.'

Fringe parties

South Africa's fringe parties ranged from the bogus to the benign. Some were motivated by fun; some were in earnest; some had difficulty in explaining themselves. All were testimony to a society with a remarkable capacity for breeding splinter groups. Almost all were destined for oblivion. But South Africa's new-found passion for airing every conceivable strain of opinion allowed each a moment or two of glory. Never before in Africa has such a motley collection of political groups been given so much attention on television, radio and in the press.

For sports and arts enthusiasts, there was the Soccer Party, formally registered as Sports Organisation for Collective Contributions and Equal Rights. Its president, James Mange, a Rastafarian musician who had once spent a year on death row and twelve years in prison for his involvement in Umkhonto we Sizwe activities, was the only leader on the ballot paper wearing dreadlocks. Soccer started off as 'the most congenial and friendly' of parties, aiming to draw people together through sports and culture, but began to project a more serious image during the course of the election campaign and ended up producing a radical tax plan.

For the ideologically minded, there was the Workers' List Party which predicted that its programme to renege on South Africa's foreign debt, nationalise big business and stage 'Nuremberg trials' for apartheid criminals would attract millions of votes. Alternatively, there was the Workers' International to Rebuild the Fourth International, a Western Cape party which advocated the revolutionary overthrow of capitalist society.

For the religiously minded, there was the African Christian Democratic Party whose slogan was: 'It's time to do it

God's way'. Or the Africa Muslim Party, whose manifesto was based on quotations from the Koran. Or the Islamic Party which advocated the legalisation of Muslim precepts like polygamy.

The ultra-right was represented by The Right Party which stood for complete separation between ethnic groups and whose leader, George Sinclair, when asked on television to explain his party's economic policies, replied that it all had to do with birth control.

Other parties included the Women's Rights Peace Party, which declared it was not 'anti-men'; the South African Women's Party, which aimed to take power out of the hands of men; and the Keep It Straight and Simple Party (Kiss), led by a Heidelberg housewife whose party emblem of a woman's lips duly appeared on the ballot paper.

The Green Party featured a marijuana leaf on the cover page of its manifesto and suggested that mass cultivation of hemp would be beneficial to the ecology and the economy. Hemp, it said, was a 'self-fertilising cash crop' that had uses ranging from the production of ethanol fuel to paper and clothing manufacture.

The Luso-South African Party aimed to capture the vote of South Africa's 500,000-strong Portuguese community but could only find two candidates.

The Minority Front was led by Amichand Rajbansi, who had been expelled from parliament on the grounds of corruption, and whom a commission of inquiry said was not fit to hold public office.

A more serious contender was the Federal Party, whose leader, Frances Kendall, the author of a number of books on federalism, liked it to be known that she had been nominated for the Nobel Peace Prize, not once but three times. The local press unkindly pointed out that being nominated was relatively easy. The Federal Party proposed the maximum devolution of powers. 'We are based on a mistrust of politicians,' Kendall explained, somewhat incongruously.

Chapter 8

The Campaign Trail

On the hustings, the centres of attention were Mandela and de Klerk. It was their names which dominated campaign activity; their roadshows which provided the greatest attraction; and their television debate which was billed as the climax of the election campaign.

The contest was not an equal one. In one township after another, from one stadium to the next, Mandela was greeted by huge exuberant crowds eager to catch a glimpse of him. For many, he was a messianic figure, the living embodiment of 80 years of struggle for political rights. Seeing Mandela was an event in itself. He made the most of his appearances, standing in open vehicles, smiling and waving in obvious pleasure, ignoring the concerns of his bodyguards in order to stretch out and shake hands, while cheerful pandemonium erupted all around. He proved to be a natural campaigner, as much at ease with crowds as with small gatherings and bystanders, with a choice of attire well-suited for each audience: flamboyant shirts for the townships, elegant striped suits for businessmen. Appearing at a mine-workers' meeting in a suit, he apologised saying that he had not had time to change into something more casual, then delighted his audience by donning a miner's helmet. White businessmen paid top prices to hear him speak.

His speeches tended to be dull and pedantic. But this mattered little, for wherever he went, in town halls, marquees or squatter camps, Mandela was already regarded as the victor of the polls and what he had to say carried with it the authority of power. When he promised jobs, housing, better education and health services, it sounded far more convincing than the same promises made by de Klerk. This confidence in the ANC's victory also enabled Mandela to confront his audiences with the unpalatable realities that most South Africans would face even when the ANC was in power. Change, he warned, must be gradual; there must be no dislocation. 'Do not expect to be driving a Mercedes the day after the elections. You must have patience. You might have to wait five years for results to show.' Narrowing the gap in income, employment and education between white and black would not be easy. Black demands for land and better living standards would have to be addressed without taking white assets. Mandela was equally forthright in upbraiding his audience for bad habits. 'If you want to continue living in unbridled poverty without clothes and food, then go and drink in shebeens. But if you want better things, you must work hard.' Addressing a tumultuous rally in Mmabatho, the capital of Bophuthatswana, a few days after the downfall of Mangope, Mandela did not mince his words in condemning looters for their 'animal behaviour'. These were expressions with which de Klerk was familiar but now felt constrained to use.

De Klerk gained a fair share of enthusiastic receptions. He moved tirelessly about the country, eager to meet people, cheerfully donning a variety of traditional dress. But the frequent disruption caused by ANC hecklers at his roadshow meetings and the conspicuous presence of nervous security officials gave him much less of a free hand. His appearances were often short, leaving crowds with expectations only half-fulfilled. His efforts to make inroads into black townships, areas he once considered 'enemy territory', were brave, but unsuccessful. The gulf in culture, language and the appalling history of his party were too great to bridge.

He found particular difficulty in putting across a coherent message. Time and again he apologised for the misery and injustice inflicted by apartheid, but then, with condescending gall, tried to claim credit for abolishing it, ignoring the role that popular struggle had played. He patronised black audiences with animal parables, notably in endeavouring to explain the difference between capitalism and socialism. If a socialist had five chickens, he said, he would eat one each day and would be left with nothing in less than a week. But a capitalist would sell the eggs. Well, maybe a capitalist would eat one or two chickens, but he certainly would not eat all of them. His audience, meanwhile, looked at him completely baffled. As well as chickens, there were bulls. The election, he said, was a contest between an old bull and a young bull. It was the National Party, as the young bull, which had a viable plan to provide more jobs, houses and better education. Warming to this theme, he added: The ANC wanted to brand the National Party as a 'white' bull, 'They say we are the party which created apartheid. This is true. We are also the party which killed apartheid. And now we are no longer the white bull. We are now a new, good Friesian.' Then there were horses. The ANC and the National Party were both 'fully grown horses'. The difference between them was that the ANC was a 'wild horse' while the National Party was a 'well-trained horse'. De Klerk's farmyard repertoire also included geese and ducks.

The main thrust of his campaign, however, was to attack the ANC, in particular its links with the South African Communist Party. The ANC was 'a dangerous party' which 'could not be trusted', he said. 'They make resounding speeches about tolerance and democracy yet their supporters practise intimidation.' They were also guilty of political violence, strikes, boycotts and disrupting education. They had no experience, no proven ability. They had yet to run a township successfully, let alone a country. Their policies of nationalisation, communism and socialism had failed everywhere else in the world. 'The ANC would cast us back into the Dark Ages. It is secretly controlled by communists, militants and extremists. They are quiet now but they will shout loudly if the ANC wins control.'

None of this appeared to make much impact on black audiences whom de Klerk needed to impress if he was to extend the National Party's support beyond its traditional white base. On home ground, he was largely preaching to the converted.

A more measured contest between the two men occurred during their debate on television before a panel of journalists. The questions they were asked and the ground over which they skirmished were largely familiar to viewers. What counted as much as content was style. De Klerk, more comfortable on television than Mandela, maintained a conciliatory countenance, admitting past wrongs, promising reconciliation, focusing on policy issues. Mandela was more aggressive, resorting to personal attacks on de Klerk's character and credibility, tending to dwell on the past evils of apartheid and sharply critical of the National Party's record.

Mandela scored well with remarks on the fact that the government was spending three times as much on a white child's education as on a black child's; that de Klerk as president paid no income tax; and with accusations that government ministers had been riding on a 'gravy train'. His repeated criticism that the National Party was trying to fan racial hatred between Coloureds and Africans in the Western Cape by distributing a picture comic book subsequently banned for its inflammatory language were highly damaging to a party trying to convince the electorate that it had shed its racist past.

De Klerk countered that the ANC had included in its list of candidates leaders of corrupt homeland governments and ANC members implicated in human rights abuses; that the ANC had been heavily involved in political violence; and that by disrupting education it was responsible for a generation of 'lost youth'.

Mandela drew attention to the merits of the ANC's reconstruction and development programme, contrasting it with the National Party's lack of a plan. De Klerk argued that an independent appraisal of the RDP showed it would cost twice as much as the ANC claimed, requiring a doubling of taxes. Mandela responded: 'This is the reply of a man not used to addressing the basic needs of the population.' He promised that his own salary as president would be cut and taxed. The political 'gravy train' would come to an end. 'We are not going to live as fat cats.' De Klerk said Mandela would get his support for frugal government, 'But if he thinks he can save on salaries of politicians to deal with the economic challenges of the country, he is in for a big surprise.'

Most of the debate was soon forgotten. What was memorable about it, however, was a dramatic gesture on Mandela's part towards the end of the debate. 'The exchanges between Mr de Klerk and I should not obscure one important fact,' he said. 'I think we are a shining example to the entire world of people drawn from different racial groups who have a common loyalty, a common love, to their common country. That is the dominating issue . . . In spite of my criticism of Mr de Klerk, sir, you are one of those I rely upon . . . We are going to face the problems of this country together.'

Reaching over to de Klerk he added: 'I am proud to hold your hand for us to go forward.'

In the cramped space of cell number seven in the maximum security block on Robben Island, Nelson Mandela demonstrated how, by standing at an angle, it was possible to wave your arms about. This was how he had exercised for 18 years.

Accompanied by five other elderly former inmates and a horde of television crews and journalists, Mandela returned to Robben Island, 30 years after being sent there to serve a life sentence, at the behest of his election campaign managers. The event was full of good humour, rarely affording a glimpse of the anguish that prisoners there suffered. Looking through the barred window of cell number seven, Mandela grinned broadly at the photographers outside, 'Could we have one serious one, please?' pleaded a photographer.

'I find it difficult to personalise the collective experience of prison,' Mandela said, 'but my advisers tell me that on this occasion I should talk about myself and not be shy.'

He spoke at length of the hardship of working in the island's lime quarry, of the isolation of his prison cell, of the stimulation of political discussions with his colleagues. Only once did he mention personal grief, in recalling the death of his mother. 'She was a completely unschooled woman ... When I practised as a lawyer I tried to support her but when I came here it was very difficult. She came to see me a couple of times. The last time was in 1968 and when she left I looked at her walking out and I had the feeling I had seen her for the last time. I cried and sought permission to go to her funeral from the authorities, but they refused. The next year my son died in a car accident and I was very hurt indeed, but again I could not pay my respects.'

But his favourite theme was the comradeship of his fellow prisoners, of their strength in adversity. Taking a stroll in the lime quarry, where he laboured until the age of 60, Mandela recalled: 'Quarry work was hard at first, but we sang freedom songs as we worked.' 'Could you sing a freedom song for us now, Mr Mandela?' asked a television journalist. He duly obliged.

Mandela also paid a visit to the gates of Victor Verster prison near Paarl, from where he had been released four years previously, laying a wreath of white flowers, lighting a 'flame of freedom' and appealing for national reconciliation. At a rally in Paarl later in the day, he expressed his appreciation of a number of white prison warders whom he had befriended.

One of them, James Gregory, had been with Mandela for 23 years, spending more time with him than any other person. On the day he was set free in 1990, Mandela wrote Gregory a note in his neat rounded handwriting: 'The wonderful hours we spent together during the last two decades end today. But you will always be in my thoughts . . .' As Mandela left, the two men shook hands and embraced.

At the National Party conference to launch its election manifesto, party delegates heralded the arrival of their leader with chants of 'Viva de Klerk! Viva!', a form of political salute copied from black politics. The delegates also gave a faltering rendition of the traditional black hymn, *Nkosi Sikelel i'Afrika*, composed at the turn of the century by a black South African cleric and long used by the African National Congress as an anthem; not many delegates were familiar with the words.

In reinventing itself, the National Party tried its best to shed its image as a white party. But the result was often surreal. The leadership remained overwhelmingly white; about two-thirds of the delegates at the conference were white; little more than one quarter of the party's candidates were black. De Klerk was defensive about the party's number of black candidates and claimed that intimidation prevented more from coming forward.

Still, at least the chairman of the proceedings, David Chuenyane, was black. A former member of the Pan-Africanist Congress who had spent years in exile, Chuenyane was asked by reporters why he had joined the National Party. 'I am an opportunist,' he replied with rare candour. 'I saw an opportunity in the NP and I said: "The NP is stranded. They need somebody black."'

Anyway, he added, 'there were no good positions going in the African National Congress.'

Amid all the razzmatazz of a Democratic Party campaign launch in the ballroom of the Carlton Hotel in Johannesburg, a black candidate stepped on to the podium to explain why she had agreed to stand for election.

'I am Sibongile Mahlangu, divorced mother of four beautiful children. Here they are. We are heading for the first election in which I will be allowed to vote. Now that all South Africans have got the right to vote, we all have the right to vote for whoever we want to.

'Last night I was woken up by a rock through my window. To all those who want to intimidate me, I want to say this: it is my democratic right to stand for the party of my choice. I have waited all my life for this moment. Don't try to take my choice away. I will stand for the DP.

'I am just an ordinary person. I don't live in a fancy house or drive a fancy car. When I am elected I will represent the voice of the ordinary people. I am proud of who I am. I am Sibongile Mahlangu.'

Venturing into a black squatter settlement near Witbank in search of votes, de Klerk was greeted by three National Party supporters wearing party hats who shook hands and briefly chatted with him outside their tin shack. Moments later, a hostile crowd of ANC supporters gathered around him, shouting abuse. 'It is our democratic right to chase him away,' explained a member of the ANC Youth League. Pointing towards the three National Party supporters, a member of the crowd said: 'Tonight, they are going to die.' Another said: 'We are going to burn that traitor and his house.' Soon after de Klerk left, the three men had to be escorted out of the settlement to safety by the police.

Irritated by the remarks of a white businessman who, during an election meeting in the civic centre in Potchefstroom, expressed concern about the number of communists involved in the ANC, Mandela responded by upbraiding his white audience for being selfish, hypocritical and racist, in the manner of a Dutch Reformed *predikant* taking a congregation of sinners to task.

The Communist Party and the ANC had fought the brutal system of apartheid together, he said. Together, members of both movements 'suffered, were harassed, arrested and thrown into prison ... Homes were broken up by a government professing to be Christian.' The Communist Party had done none of these things. 'You Christians have done them. Why should we listen to you about our comrades in the Communist Party? Is this not a sign of selfishness on your part? You have the temerity to come to me ... [expecting that] I will say to an ally with whom we have fought and suffered that we will now abandon them, on the verge of victory – on your instructions. You, who have no concern for me.' Apartheid, he said, had been inflicted on masses of people by a 'community which claimed to be committed to religious values ... You must stand ashamed. Your community used the word of God to justify [apartheid].'

In a dramatic return to the centre of South African politics, Winnie Mandela, disgraced as a result of her criminal conviction for kidnapping, her publicised affair with a young ANC lawyer and allegations over misappropriated ANC funds, was unexpectedly elected president of the ANC's Women's League at a conference in Durban in December, 1993. The return of Winnie came as a disagreeable surprise to several prominent ANC figures who had assumed that her forced resignation from all ANC posts the year before had settled her fate, and gave some indication of both her unrelenting ambition and her skill at gaining support in squatter compounds and amongst the youth. Not once did she show any trace of remorse over her involvement in the kidnapping of a 14-year-old boy who was later murdered, nor over the activities of her bodyguard, the Mandela Football Club, which, press investigations alleged, was linked to a number of other murders.

The National Party was quick to take advantage of the event. Full-page newspaper advertisements appeared containing a large photograph of Winnie Mandela, her right arm raised in a clenched fist salute, with a three-paragraph commentary beneath which said: 'On 10 July 1993 Winnie Mandela was convicted of kidnapping a child who later died from his wounds. On 8 December 1993 she was elected to be the most powerful woman in the ANC, the president of the ANC's Women's League. After 27 April 1994, Mrs Mandela could be your new Minister of Law and Order, or even the Minister of Child Welfare ... Only your vote can stop this.'

A sign of the extent of Winnie's popularity came when she was chosen fifth in order of preference on a list of nominations for candidates for parliament put forward by ANC members nationwide. An ANC electoral college prudently removed her to thirty-first place in the final list.

A number of unsavoury characters found their way on to candidates lists. The National Party's national list for Natal included a former Indian member of the House of Delegates who had been sentenced to death in Ireland for killing and dismembering his 15-year-old girlfriend, but released after seven years' imprisonment. Its list for the Western Cape legislature included two *'witdoek'* warlords whose followers had been responsible for the mass destruction of squatter camps on the Cape flats leaving scores dead and thousands homeless.

The ANC's list included a former guerrilla convicted of killing three young women in a bomb attack outside a bar on Durban's beachfront; three other Umkhonto members implicated by an ANC commission of inquiry into torture in ANC detention camps in Angola and involvement in human rights abuses; and the heads of two homeland governments which had been indicted publicly for massive corruption.

The Democratic Party made the most of this in its election advertisements. 'If you vote for the ANC or the Nats, you'll be entrusting people like these with your future.' Its street posters read: 'No killers. No kidnappers. No torturers. And no corrupt politicians.'

One prospective candidate who failed to find a place on a party list was a mass-murderer named Barend Strydom. In 1988, Strydom, a former policeman, went on a killing spree in central Pretoria, firing indiscriminately at black people, wounding 22 and killing eight, smiling as he did so. At his trial, he said he went on the rampage 'to show the world there were Boers on the southern tip of Africa who would fight for the maintenance of Christian Calvinism and fight communism'. Blacks, he said, threatened the survival of the white race. 'Each black person threatens the continued existence of whites, even an 88-year-old woman. They are known to breed very fast. Scientists have shown that the oxygen is decreasing. This is the fault of blacks. They are threatening the life of the entire planet.'

Sentenced to death in 1988, released from prison in 1992 as part of a general amnesty, Strydom surfaced during the election campaign, offering his services as a candidate to General Viljoen's Freedom Front. His offer was declined. A spokesman said the party did not accept 'just anybody'.

Prisoners launched their own election campaign – staging hunger strikes, seizing hostages and setting fire to cells in several days of rioting – demanding that all inmates should be allowed to vote. Under election regulations, prisoners guilty of murder, rape, kidnapping and other serious crimes were excluded from voting, but minor offenders were given the right to vote. A campaign started by a former prisoner named Golden Miles Bhudu, who specialised in making appearances at public functions wreathed in heavy chains to publicise prisoners' grievances, urged inmates to take action.

After a group of 21 prisoners were burned to death in a fire in Queenstown jail, an unseemly squabble broke out in the Transitional Executive Council about what to do. The ANC favoured giving all prisoners the vote. The Democratic Party reluctantly agreed. The government, however, refused to go along and made much capital out of the fact. A National Party advertisement appeared in the press featuring an identikit of a notorious serial killer known as the 'Station Strangler', who was still on the loose at the time in the Cape Town area, with the heading: 'Can you imagine the Cape Strangler having the vote? The ANC and DP can.' The advertisement had considerable impact among the Coloured community in Cape Town from whom his victims had come.

The Coloured community in the Cape – apartheid's 'step-children' – found itself the subject of unaccustomed attention during the campaign. Though Coloureds constituted no more than ten per cent of the electorate at a national level, in the Western Cape they were the largest single group, numbering more than two million, about 57 per cent of the electorate there; and in the Northern Cape, numbering 260,000, they made up nearly 60 per cent of the electorate. The Coloured vote, therefore, was to be a decisive factor in determining the outcome of both regions' elections. Mandela and de Klerk spent more time wooing Coloured voters in the Cape than anywhere else.

As much the victims of apartheid as Africans, Coloureds had no reason to show any liking for the National Party. In the 1950s, it had stripped them of their right to vote; in the 1960s, it had forced them, under the Group Areas Act, to move out of areas such as District Six in Cape Town, where they had lived for generations, in order to make way for white occupation; in the 1970s, it continued to ignore Coloured interests – 'non-people' was how de Klerk's wife, Marike, once described Coloureds in a newspaper interview.

Yet ties of language, culture and religion to the Afrikaner community kept most Coloureds in closer touch with whites than with Africans. Some 80 per cent spoke Afrikaans at home. Though most Coloured voters disdained the opportunity to participate in elections to the House of Representatives when it was set up as part of the tricameral system in the 1980s, the benefits of the system eventually appeared in the form of 100,000 houses and 100 secondary schools for Coloureds. National Party policy began to stress the importance of ties between the white and Coloured communities. In 1993, the first Coloureds were given portfolios in the National Party cabinet.

As the 1994 election approached, Coloureds showed distinct signs of apprehension about the possibility of an ANC victory. The ANC was perceived to be a party favouring black interests, at the expense not just of white interests but also of Coloured interests. The rapid African influx into Cape Town during the 1980s had already aroused fears that blacks would try to take Coloured jobs. These fears were now aggravated by the ANC's plans for affirmative action which many Coloureds believed would apply only to blacks, even though Mandela reassured them that they would include all disadvantaged groups. Fears were also expressed that blacks would take over Coloured housing; examples of the illegal occupation by Africans of Coloured housing were readily cited. Mandela's assurances that 'your homes will be safe under an ANC government' were to no avail. Opinion polls noted a sharp increase in Coloured hostility towards the prospect of black rule. Many Coloureds expressed the view that the country would be better off if whites continued to run it and that blacks would only 'make a mess' of it.

The National Party did its best to exploit these fears. It produced a picture comic book, especially aimed at Coloured youth in townships on the Cape Flats, featuring a discussion between a student and his parents on whether to vote for the National Party in the election, in which the ANC was blamed for the violence sweeping the country, setting black against black and brother against brother. 'The liberators have become the killers; they shout freedom and sow death.' Under an ANC government, people could expect to hear the slogan 'Kill a Coloured, Kill a farmer'. After the ANC lodged a complaint with an independent electoral tribunal claiming the comic was 'provocative and inflammatory', the National Party was ordered to withdraw all copies of the comic.

Once renowned for its more relaxed racial attitudes, the Cape Town area witnessed rising racial tension during the election campaign. 'This is territory where the word "kaffir" is bandied about more liberally than in ultra-conservative Ventersdorp [in western Transvaal],' wrote a visiting black journalist.

The beneficiary of all this was de Klerk. He acquired a hero's status among the Coloured community with a popularity rating of 62 per cent. Mandela, though claiming Cape Town as his 'home' in view of the 27 years he had spent in jail in the area, languished behind with no more than 17 per cent.

*

The Pan-Africanist Congress, whose main policy was to expropriate all land without compensation and whose record of murderous attacks was still fresh in the public mind, announced in March that the party was broke, its officials were living from hand to mouth, and its office telephone had been disconnected. The PAC's president, Clarence Makwetu, blamed the party's problems on the business and international communities, accusing them of withholding funding from the PAC while supporting the ANC. 'Big business and the overseas community is determined to ensure that these are one-sided elections,' he complained. 'Our efforts to get the same kind of assistance have fallen on deaf ears. We know that our policies have been grossly misunderstood by big business at home and abroad.'

Among the rumours floated during the election campaign, the most bizarre was started by Transkei's military dictator, General Bantubonke Holomisa. Holomisa had a reputation for making senseless remarks, but during the election campaign what he had to say was accorded greater significance by virtue of the fact that he was placed at number 13 on the ANC's national list of candidates.

Holomisa claimed that the National Party intended to rig the vote by putting invisible ink, due to be used in the polling process to indicate voters who had already cast their ballots, into maize porridge and feeding this to black voters, thereby disqualifying them from voting.

Holomisa was duly found guilty by an election tribunal of contravening the electoral code of conduct.

An ambitious plan to establish a 'National Peacekeeping Force', dreamt up by negotiators at the World Trade Centre as a way of providing impartial peace-keeping during the run-up to the election, turned into a long-running fiasco, culminating in disaster when the force was first deployed two weeks before the election date.

The idea was that various 'armed formations' – the army, police, Umkhonto and homeland security forces – would contribute personnel to the NPKF to be trained for deployment in volatile areas such as the East Rand where units like the paramilitary police force's Internal Stability Division were regarded as hostile by local residents.

The NPKF was flawed from the start. Inkatha's refusal to participate in the NPKF undermined its legitimacy as a neutral force at a stroke. By being able to claim that the NPKF was effectively a front for Umkhonto, Inkatha ensured that any deployment in areas of conflict would involve high risk.

The appointment of its commander was highly controversial. After months of squabbling, the army and Umkhonto chose Brigadier Gabriel Ramushwana, the military dictator of Venda who was already standing as an ANC candidate in the election. Not only did this further undermine the NPKF's hopes to be accepted as a neutral force, but Ramushwana at the time was at the centre of a massive pension fund scandal, making him a particularly inept choice. Thousands of Venda civil servants embarked on a mass action protest against his appointment, demanding that he first be required to answer allegations of corruption back home.

The time available for training and for drawing together units from disparate backgrounds, expertise, tradition and training was no more than six weeks. Umkhonto personnel, who made up about half the initial number of NPKF recruits, had no previous experience of riot control or other peace-keeping duties. Many of them turned out to be undisciplined and unsuited for the job. Two weeks after its formation, NPKF instructors reported a collapse of discipline, desertion, drunkenness and anti-white racism. In one incident, a group of drunken soldiers started chanting ANC revolutionary songs – 'Kill the boer, Kill the farmer' – and threatening officers.

The catalogue of disorder continued. NPKF recruits went on strike, demanding higher pay. The Transitional Executive Council capitulated, setting off a wave of other demands from police and civil servants for higher pay. The Chief of Staff was dismissed summarily after being charged with drunk driving. A battalion commander faced a charge of culpable homicide resulting from a motor vehicle accident. Two other members were arrested for murder. In all, some 1,000 members were dismissed. Professional officers brought in to evaluate the NPKF warned that it was not ready for deployment.

Ignoring all the danger signs, politicians on the Transitional Executive Council took the decision to deploy the NPKF to the East Rand townships, for several years the scene of running battles between the ANC's 'self-defence units' and Inkatha hostel dwellers.

Since February 1994, as the result of skilful operations carried out by the South African Defence Force, the East Rand townships had been largely pacified. But the potential for violence was never far from the surface. Within days of taking over from the SADF, the NPKF was involved in a series of gun-battles in Thokosa. NPKF were reported to have held their commander hostage, disobeyed orders, panicked under fire, consumed alcohol on duty and shot at the police. Their random fire was also said to have been responsible for the death of an award-winning photographer, Ken Oosterbroek.

The NPKF was subsequently transferred to non-operational duties.

Even before they started, officials charged with running the Independent Electoral Commission regarded the completion of the task as daunting if not impossible, but, as the political terrain on which they were working continued to shift, their difficulties multiplied far beyond their worst expectations.

In four months, the IEC had to recruit 250,000 people; train them in election procedures; organise voter education programmes for millions of people, many of them illiterate; ensure that millions obtained identity documents; monitor election meetings; mediate election disputes; assist free electioneering; handle thousands of enquiries; and deal with complaints and contraventions of electoral law from all quarters. Polling stations had to be identified without reliable demographic data or electoral rolls.

In February 1994 the change from the use of one ballot paper to two ballot papers per person meant not only a doubling of the administrative load but a redesign of all polling stations.

The worst difficulties were encountered when homeland authorities in Bophuthatswana and KwaZulu refused to collaborate. Bophuthatswana's resistance was overcome with the fall of Mangope in March. But Buthelezi held out until a week before the election. Because of the security threat, large areas of KwaZulu had been left uncovered. With only seven days remaining, the IEC was suddenly required to set up and man an extra 500 polling stations. Buthelezi's late participation also meant printing special stickers for Inkatha which had to be affixed to more than 40 million ballot papers.

In a confident burst of advertisements urging people to vote, the IEC proclaimed: 'We are ready. You are ready. Let's do it.'

In the event, everybody was ready but the IEC.

The last weeks of white rule came in a rush of excitement, anxiety and sheer chaos. Like a fever, strikes over pay and pensions spread through homeland administrations bringing them to the point of collapse. Nurses abandoned hospitals in Transkei, Venda, Lebowa, Gazankulu and KwaZulu. Police, magistrates, ambulancemen and civil servants joined in the protests. In Transkei, transport workers took their managers hostage; and prison staff locked out senior wardens. Veterans of the ANC's mass action campaigns, Joe Slovo and Cyril Ramaphosa, were left to plead with strikers to return to work 'in the national interest'. At a ceremony marking Transkei's reincorporation into South Africa, its military dictator, General Holomisa, commented on the mood of gloom which pervaded the homeland. 'It is ironic that people who are on the verge of emancipation from the ruthless tentacles of racial domination and oppression should be sad and oppressed.'

Rumours of impending doom swept through parts of the white community. Pamphlets and facsimiles circulated warning of disruption to power and water supplies and provided a 'keep alive list' covering everything from drinking water to toilet paper as well as giving advice on how to douse petrol-bomb fires. A list issued by the right-wing Conservative Party recommended that a survival kit should include 'arms and ammunition, a small Bible, and a panga or small axe'. Even the South African Chamber of Business suggested to members they should be prepared for the worst.

Supermarkets, corner cafés and farm co-operatives were stripped of canned food, candles, rice, long-life milk, batteries and primus stoves. Whites in the northern suburbs of Johannesburg queued for hours to fill gas cylinders. Gun dealers could hardly keep up with the demand. Newspapers reported airline flights to Lisbon, Tel Aviv and a number of European destinations were booked solid for months ahead. Plans for mass evacuation were said to be in hand.

Right-wing parties readily fanned the flames of fear. The Afrikaner Weerstandsbeweging issued a statement predicting 'chaos, uprising and revolution' after the election and claimed that 'thousands of members' were moving into western Transvaal to 'ward off' persecution expected from the new government. Some right-wingers quit their jobs and left their homes in other areas to move there.

In the agricultural town of Viljoenskroon in the Orange Free State, AWB members set up a *laager* of barbed-wire fences, road blocks and military watch-towers on access roads to the town – in order to keep blacks out. The local traffic police chief, supervising the construction of road booms, spoke of the fate of Piet Retief, a famous *voortrekker* killed by blacks in the nineteenth century. 'You can't trust them,' he said. 'This election is history coming back after 150 years. Just look what happened to Piet Retief.' When the security forces made clear their disapproval of the fortifications, the local town council agreed to take them down.

Thus the old order passed away.

Chapter 9

The Election Result

The pattern of voting followed a predictable course. The vast bulk of the black electorate provided the ANC and Nelson Mandela with a handsome victory. A majority in the white, Coloured and Indian communities held fast to the National Party and de Klerk. Zulu nationalists voted, in larger numbers than expected, for Inkatha and Buthelezi. Afrikaner nationalists, hoping for a *volkstaat*, put their trust in the Freedom Front, but in smaller numbers than General Viljoen had hoped. A diminished band of white liberals voted for the Democratic Party. And an insignificant rump of black radicals voted for the Pan-Africanist Congress.

At a national level, the ANC obtained 62.6 per cent of the vote, taking 12,237,600 of the 19,530,000 valid votes cast, and gaining 252 seats in the 400-seat National Assembly. At a provincial level, it gained outright control of six of the nine provincial assemblies, taking, in the Northern Transvaal, 38 of 40 seats (91.6 per cent of the vote); in the Eastern Transvaal, 25 of 30 seats (80.7 per cent); in the North West, 26 of 30 seats (83.3 per cent); in the Orange Free State, 24 of 30 seats (76.6 per cent); in PWV, 50 of 86 seats (57.6 per cent); and in the Eastern Transvaal, 48 of 56 seats (84.4 per cent). In the Northern Cape, it gained 15 of 30 seats (49.7 per cent). In the two remaining provinces, Western Cape (33.0 per cent) and KwaZulu/Natal (32.2 per cent), it failed to gain control. The result showed that the ANC, despite its multiracial leadership, collected a mainly black vote, with some support from the Coloured community, but virtually none from the white community.

The National Party, despite its attempts to find support among the black electorate, remained a stronghold of the white and Coloured communities. At a national level, it obtained 20.4 per cent of the poll, collecting 3,983,000 votes, and gaining 82 seats in the National Assembly. At the provincial level, because of Coloured support, it gained 23 of 42 seats in Western Cape (53.2 per cent), and twelve of 30 seats in Northern Cape (40.5 per cent). In the PWV province, it gained 21 of 86 seats (23.9 per cent).

Inkatha's performance was stronger than expected, but the result showed it to be an ethnically based party, dependent on Zulu support within KwaZulu/Natal. Inkatha gained 10.5 per cent of the national poll, taking 43 seats in the National Assembly; but its 2,058,000 votes came overwhelmingly from KwaZulu/Natal. It also gained a majority in the provincial assembly in KwaZulu/Natal, taking 41 of 81 seats, leaving the ANC trailing with 26 seats and the National Party with nine seats. But outside KwaZulu/Natal, the only province where it won a following sufficient to obtain representation was in PWV where it took three of 81 seats.

The fourth largest party, General Viljoen's Freedom Front, obtained only 2.17 per cent of the national poll, with 424,500 votes, giving it nine seats in the National Assembly. Its showing at the provincial level, in terms of the total votes cast, was higher: it collected 640,000 votes. But its following was too widely dispersed to bring the idea of a *volkstaat* any closer to reality. In provincial assemblies it gained one seat in Northern Transvaal; two seats in Eastern Transvaal; one seat in North West; two seats in Orange Free State; five seats in PWV; two seats in Northern Cape; and one seat in Western Cape.

The Democratic Party clung to survival with 1.7 per cent of the national poll, winning no more than 338,400 votes, and only seven seats in the National Assembly. In none of the provinces did it show a significant following.

The Pan-Africanist Congress fared even worse, collecting 1.2 per cent of the national poll, with 243,400 votes and five seats in the National Assembly. Its future seemed in doubt.

Of the fringe parties, only the African Christian Democratic Party survived, with 0.5 per cent of the national vote, giving it two seats in the National Assembly.

The overall result was in line with public expectations and accepted by all political parties. The fact that Inkatha gained control of the KwaZulu/Natal provincial legislature, rather than the ANC, defused what otherwise might rapidly have turned into another round of political warfare and gave Buthelezi sufficient standing to participate in the new dispensation without harbouring grievances. The ANC's reward of national control was large enough to keep its Natal supporters in line. The fact that the ANC failed to cross the two-thirds threshold of the national vote, which would have given it power to write the final constitution on its own, helped to still minority fears that it would be tempted to ride roughshod over their interests. But the party was still left well satisfied with the result.

In all quarters, however, there were deep misgivings about the conduct of the election by the Independent Electoral Commission. The IEC's performance was at times so incompetent that it threatened the whole electoral process. But for emergency intervention by the army and air force during the course of voting – providing aircraft, helicopters, vehicles and other logistical facilities – the consequences would have been calamitous. Even so, thousands of homeland residents stood waiting patiently at polling stations for three days and never got to vote at all because of the shortage of ballot papers and other equipment. An emergency one-day extension of voting, in addition to the three days already allocated, was needed for six areas to prevent thousands more from being effectively disenfranchised. Millions of extra ballot papers had to be printed at the last minute. Security procedures were abandoned one after another. Desperate election officials, faced with a shortage of ballot boxes, resorted to opening full ballot boxes and emptying their contents into other containers so that they could be used again. The opportunities for electoral fraud proliferated. Days of chaos at polling stations were followed by days of chaos at counting stations. To keep the counting process moving, the IEC jettisoned all efforts to reconcile the numbers of ballots issued to the numbers returned. 'This election is not about vote reconciliation,' proclaimed Judge Kriegler, head of the IEC, 'It is about national conciliation.' Complaints and irregularities soon swamped the IEC from every quarter. Rumours of massive electoral fraud in KwaZulu/Natal circulated. One week after the voting had stopped, representatives of political parties were engaged in what was described as 'horse-trading' over election disputes and irregularities. 'Let's not get overly squeamish about it,' remarked Kriegler. At the end of it all, Kriegler pronounced the election 'substantially free and fair', though flawed. Irregularities had not affected the overall result. The findings of international observers from the European Union, the Commonwealth and other missions were similar.

Rising above all the muddle and confusion was the clear verdict of the people. By voting in their millions, free from intimidation and from violence and with great dignity, South Africans ensured the triumph of democracy. The election was not so much a battle of ideas or policies: little divided the policy objectives of rival political parties; their arguments were more about the past than the future. The election was essentially about liberation: for blacks voting for the first time, a celebration of their freedom; for whites, a celebration that South Africa itself was now free.

That the transfer of power was accomplished in an atmosphere of so much goodwill, after such a long and bitter conflict, was due in large measure to the leadership of two remarkable South Africans, de Klerk and Mandela, and to the fortitude of the people they represented. Four years earlier, South Africa had been moving inexorably towards violent revolution. What de Klerk and Mandela had achieved since was to ensure that the revolution was a peaceful one.

As he closed the book on three centuries of white rule, de Klerk chose words of encouragement, fitting for such a historic moment. 'Mr Mandela has walked a long road and now stands at the top of the hill. A man of destiny knows that beyond this hill lies another and another. The journey is never complete. As he contemplates the next hill, I hold out my hand to Mr Mandela in friendship and co-operation.'

Chapter 10

Profiles

Nelson Mandela, President

After 50 years as a political activist, welding together a nationalist movement to defeat white rule, Nelson Mandela now faces a task of even greater magnitude. From the moment he took office on 10 May 1994, the crisis of expectation was upon him.

Mandela's achievement in engineering a negotiated revolution in collaboration with South Africa's white rulers is that it left intact an administration both powerful enough and sufficiently amenable to undertake the ambitious targets he has set for his government and which an impatient electorate expects him to deliver.

The degree of confidence with which the old white establishment regards Mandela's government is due in large measure to the presence of familiar figures like de Klerk in the cabinet and the guarantees given it under the new constitution. It is also the result of the sustained efforts that Mandela has made to reassure whites of the value he places on their role in a new South Africa. Even from prison, as his 1989 memorandum shows, Mandela was at pains to address the question of white fears of black rule. Upon his release from 27 years of imprisonment, he called for a generosity of spirit on the part of blacks in allaying those fears. On the day he voted, on 27 April 1994, he spoke of the need to give the white minority 'confidence and security'. It is a sign of how far he has succeeded in addressing white concerns that many whites have now come to express apprehension about his passing.

The personal qualities which Mandela brought to bear in the struggle against white rule were remarkable. There were times during his years in prison – 'these long, lonely, wasted years', he wrote in 1985 – when he doubted whether the cause of democracy would ever succeed. The worst moments came as a result of the government's persecution of his own family. 'To see your family, your children, being persecuted when you are absolutely helpless in jail, that is one of the most bitter experiences, most painful experiences, I have had,' he said in April 1994. 'Your wife being hounded from job to job, your children being taken out of Coloured schools, police breaking into your house at midnight and even assaulting your wife.' Yet not once did Mandela express bitterness towards the white community for his ordeal, only against the system they imposed. Saying farewell to the white prison warder whom he had known for 23 years, Mandela embraced him with tears in his eyes. 'The wonderful hours we spent together during the last two decades end today,' he wrote in a note, 'but you will always be in my thoughts.'

Mandela's moral stature stood out all the more in an age bereft of political morality. His natural authority and charisma were evident to all who encountered him, and he possessed a winning smile to boot. Foreign leaders were only too keen to be seen in his company to enhance their own respectability. His inauguration as president in May 1994 was attended by one of the most glittering assemblies of heads of state, royalty and government leaders ever seen, as much in tribute to Mandela as to South Africa's rite of passage. 'The world's last authentic hero' was the description accorded him by a Philadelphia newspaper.

Mandela enjoyed the fame, but was unmoved by it. He remained courteous and attentive to individuals, whatever their status or their age. He would often stop to talk to children or young adults, with genuine interest. His manners were punctilious, reminiscent of another, more gracious, age. Despite his patrician bearing, he possessed the common touch, taking care to greet workers or tycoons with the same civility. The chores of everyday life were not beneath him, as he explained to an election meeting: 'I make my own bed. I can cook a decent meal. I can polish a floor,' he said, adding, to the delight of women in the audience, that men should undertake more domestic tasks. 'Why can't you do it?'

An intensely private man, hardened by prison experience, he allows few glimpses of his private life, preferring to talk instead about the movement or the party, his place in the team rather than his position as leader. Almost all his adult life has been taken up by the struggle for political rights. As his old friend, Oliver Tambo, once recalled: 'We were never really young. There were no dances, hardly a cinema, but meetings, discussions, every night, every weekend.' So it continued year after year, from the hectic days of the Youth League in the 1940s, to the Defiance Campaign, the Congress of the People, and the Treason Trial of the 1950s. His marriage to Winnie in 1958 occurred amid the same blur of activity. They fell deeply in love, but spent little time together.

Mandela's decision to commit the ANC to armed rebellion in the 1960s was based on a fatal miscalculation about the nature of white power. The sabotage campaign, which led to his sentence for life imprisonment, never had the slightest chance of success. It merely enabled a government ruthless in its use of power to crush the rebellion in the name of law and order and to silence black opposition for more than a decade.

Yet the reasons that Mandela gave for his decision were clear enough and articulated with such eloquence at his trial in 1964 that they stood as a powerful indictment of white rule which resounded down the years. 'It was only when all else had failed, when all channels of peaceful protest had been barred to us, that the decision was made to embark on violent forms of political struggle, and to form Umkhonto we Sizwe. We did so not because we desired such a course, but solely because the government had left us with no other choice.'

Even more memorable was the statement of his personal beliefs at the trial, which, in time, came to be quoted so often that it reached biblical proportions. 'During my lifetime I have dedicated myself to this struggle of the African people. I have fought against black domination and I have fought against white domination. I have cherished the ideal of a democratic and free society in which all persons live together in harmony and with equal opportunities. It is an ideal which I hope to live for and achieve. But if needs be it is an ideal for which I am prepared to die.'

The extent of Mandela's ordeal was never forgotten by the people for whom he spoke and duly remembered when the time came for them, in their millions, to cast their vote. The victory of the ANC at the polls in 1994 was as much a personal tribute to Mandela as it was to the movement he led. Time and again it was said: 'He went to prison for us.'

Once asked how different was the man who emerged from prison to the one who went in, he replied: 'I came out mature.' The change from the young Mandela was marked indeed. Oliver Tambo once described him as 'passionate, emotional, sensitive, quickly stung to bitterness and retaliation by insult and patronage'. In prison he came to understand that bitterness would achieve nothing, would leave him no closer to his goal. He emerged distrustful of emotion, prizing reason and logic above all else, as his didactic manner now betrays. The life of austerity and discipline to which he became accustomed he still maintains. He rises early each day, spending the pre-dawn hours on an exercise bike, in the same way that he used to wave his arms about in his prison cell. He neither drinks nor smokes, and never swears. By temperament, he tends to be autocratic.

Amid the triumph there is a sense of sadness about Mandela's life, not just because of the suffering that was endured, but because, even after his release, personal happiness seemed to evade him. Mandela was never under any illusion about what sacrifice was required. Speaking at his first trial, in 1962, about his decision to leave home and family for an underground existence, constantly hunted by police, he remarked: 'No man in his right senses would voluntarily choose such a life in preference to the one of normal, family social life which exists in every civilised country. But there comes a time, as it came in my life, when a man is denied the right to live a normal life, when he can only live the life of an outlaw because the government has so decreed to use the law to impose a state of outlawry upon him.'

Yet the normal, family social life for which he so longed he never found again. The wayward conduct of his wife, Winnie, the scandal of her involvement in the notorious bodyguard known as the Mandela Football Club, her criminal conviction for kidnapping, her infidelity, all blighted Mandela's late years of freedom. Still deeply in love, he blamed himself for being unable to protect her from the persecution inflicted upon her year after year by a vengeful government, by which he explained her behaviour. But it was no consolation. Moving away to live in the northern suburbs of Johannesburg, he became a solitary figure, admired, respected and much loved, but standing alone and once again surrounded by armed guards. Now, in his seventy-fifth year, when he would prefer to spend more time with his grandchildren, he faces the Herculean task of nation-building.

Government of National Unity

The Government of National Unity, which Mandela leads, is a curious hybrid. It consists of communists and anti-communists, capitalists and anti-capitalists, liberal democrats and social democrats, several Zulu nationalists and a chartered accountant on whom much attention is centred. A sense of continuity is provided by the presence of de Klerk, as a Deputy President, and of Derek Keys, a successful businessman who was appointed Minister of Finance in 1992 and who retains the post under Mandela. A former chartered accountant, Keys is highly regarded as a financial manager by the business community both at home and abroad. His appointment signifies Mandela's commitment to economic discipline, but his fate is to become a punchbag, under continual pressure to produce more money than is available.

A sense of change comes with the team Mandela has installed. Mandela wants rapid change and rapid results. But he will be constantly hampered by the shortage of resources to produce them.

It was something of a political miracle which brought so many disparate politicians together into a Government of National Unity. It will be something of a political miracle if they all manage to pull together in the same direction. Yet there is a common understanding of the urgent need to provide more jobs and housing if disillusionment and social unrest are to be avoided. The focus of attention, therefore, will fall on those ministers charged with implementing key aspects of the new government's reconstruction and development programme.

Thabo Mbeki, Deputy President

During the ANC's years as a revolutionary movement, Thabo Mbeki came to be seen in the West as its acceptable face. An accomplished politician, urbane and articulate, he was a central figure in the ANC's campaign to promote economic sanctions against Pretoria and to gain diplomatic recognition and support for the movement in exile. He ended up, as head of its department for international affairs, running a larger number of 'embassies' than Pretoria did.

He was also skilful in handling contacts with the

ever-increasing stream of South Africans – businessmen, academics and churchmen – who travelled from South Africa in the 1980s to talk to the ANC in defiance of the government, seeking ways out of the impasse. Mbeki, they found, puffing on his ubiquitous pipe, spoke more the language of the middle class than the rhetoric expected of revolutionaries. Once back in South Africa from exile, he performed much the same task, pacifying businessmen alarmed by talk of nationalisation.

Mbeki comes from a distinguished political family. His father, Govan Mbeki, is a former ANC National Chairman who was sentenced to life imprisonment with Mandela at the Rivonia trial. Thabo Mbeki joined the ANC Youth League in 1956 at the age of 14 and, after the ANC was banned in 1960, worked underground, mobilising student and youth protests, before leaving South Africa in 1962.

During his 28 years of exile, he studied economics at the University of Sussex, in England, underwent military training in the Soviet Union, represented the ANC in London, Botswana, Swaziland, Nigeria and Zambia, before joining the staff of Oliver Tambo and then taking over as head of party's international affairs in 1989.

In 1993, following the death of Oliver Tambo, Mbeki was elected as ANC National Chairman, a position which placed him at number three in the hierarchy after Mandela and the Deputy President, Walter Sisulu. Support for Mbeki in the election came, surprisingly in view of Mbeki's reputation as a moderate, from the ANC's Youth League and, in particular, its leader, Peter Mokaba, well known for his extremist stance and liking for slogans like 'Kill the boer, Kill the farmer'.

Now in line to follow Mandela as South Africa's next president, Mbeki manages to bridge the gap between radical and moderate factions, retaining a sharp social conscience but remaining pragmatic.

Jay Naidoo, Minister without Portfolio, in charge of Reconstruction and Development Programme

Saying farewell to the trade union federation, Cosatu, where he had spent eight years as general secretary, Jay Naidoo left for the heady world of politics in late 1993 with the words: 'I pledge to you that we will not allow ourselves to be manipulated by any government.' It was one of the many contradictory positions that ANC leaders found themselves in as they made the change from the politics of resistance to the business of government.

As minister in charge of the government's reconstruction and development programme, Naidoo requires considerable personal powers of manipulation to coax South Africa towards the objectives it has set and which, as co-ordinator, he played a large part in drawing up. Once the scourge of big business, he now needs the co-operation of big business to maintain progress towards those objectives. He denies that the RDP is hostile towards private-sector interests. 'On the contrary, we painstakingly sought to assess and encourage the role of the private sector. We considered what firms and financial institutions can reasonably be expected to contribute to the programme without undue risk, diminished profits or outright losses.'

For their part, businessmen have mostly come to respect Naidoo's ability as a negotiator and as an administrator. In an opinion poll of 100 business leaders published in December 1993, some 47 per cent responded positively when asked about his possible appointment as a cabinet minister, using words like 'talented', 'articulate' and 'astute'; 25 per cent had mixed feelings; and 27 per cent responded negatively. Far harsher words were used uniformly about Naidoo during his career as a trade union leader.

Coming from a poor family in Durban, which was evicted from their home under the Group Areas Act when he was four years old, Naidoo developed a strong commitment to working-class interests. As general secretary of Cosatu from its formation in 1985, he built it into a formidable vehicle not just for use in promoting workers' interests but in the wider anti-apartheid struggle.

He asserts he will not lend his influence with the unions to help keep them in line. 'I will never be used by a future democratic government to try to control the trade union movement.' But equally he argues that the unions must not expect their representatives in parliament solely to take up union interests. 'Cosatu must pursue an independent programme at a mass level and through negotiations to get what it wants and to defend its constituency's interests.'

Naidoo's basic objective is to assure some 'minimal life-line service to all South Africans' within a reasonable period of time. 'We are inheriting a country with massive unemployment, a serious housing shortage, lack of a skilled workforce, a huge pool of poorly educated people, and a host of other imbalances that need to be redressed to satisfy the ordinary man in the street.'

Joe Slovo, Minister of Housing

Joe Slovo has exerted a powerful influence on the African National Congress and the South African Communist Party for more than 40 years. His fingerprints can be found on landmark documents like the Freedom Charter of 1955, the interim constitution of 1993 and the ANC's Reconstruction and Development Programme. During the 27 years he spent in exile, he provided a key link for the ANC in obtaining Soviet support, and, as chief of staff of Umkhonto we Sizwe, he was largely responsible for military as well as political strategy. His commitment to socialism has remained unswerving. Yet he has also used his influence to support crucial compromises upon which agreement on the interim constitution was based, disdaining the arguments of radical activists in favour of hardline positions. He has proved as adept on the platform at public meetings as in the negotiating chamber and is greeted as a popular figure in the townships. Mandela regards him as a trusted adviser, 'one of our finest patriots', as he described Slovo on the day he left prison. But Slovo's illness from bone marrow cancer is likely to curtail the extent of his activity.

Like the arch-ideologue, Hendrik Verwoerd, Slovo was not born in South Africa, but emigrated there from Lithuania with his parents at the age of nine in 1935. Obliged to leave school when he was 15, he worked as a clerk, became involved in trade union activities and joined the Young Communist League in Yeoville, a suburb of Johannesburg. During World War II he saw action in Egypt and Italy. Upon his return he studied law at the University of the Witwatersrand, graduating in 1950, and took up work as a defence lawyer in political trials, all the while pursuing his activities as a member of the Communist Party. Together with his wife, Ruth First, also a leading communist intellectual, he was 'named' under the Suppression of Communism Act of 1950 and subjected to restrictions.

Nevertheless his political work continued unabated. As a founding member of the Congress of Democrats, launched in 1953, he was involved in the planning of the Congress of the People and contributed to the drafting of the Freedom Charter. Charged with treason in 1956, along with other activists, he served as a member of the defence team. The charges against him were dropped in 1958. A high-ranking member of Umkhonto, he was abroad in 1963 when police raided its headquarters at Lilliesleaf Farm, Rivonia, and remained there.

In exile, Slovo was portrayed by the South African government as one of its most sinister and dangerous opponents, a KGB colonel dedicated to the overthrow of white rule. He was indeed notable for his rigid loyalty to the Soviet Union, a confirmed Stalinist ready to parrot the party line whenever duty called. 'For there to be a personality cult, there had to be worshippers and I was a worshipper,' he said in 1988. He was equally committed to revolutionary war against Pretoria. For years, his pamphlet, *No Middle Road*, served as a standard guide for all would-be revolutionaries.

Yet his time in exile was often bleak and barren. 'Exile life for 27 years had its moments even of hopelessness,' Slovo later recalled. 'There were moments when one thought, "How long, oh Lord?" We were really destroyed as a force for quite a long time. Between 1963 and about 1978 no shot was fired in anger in South Africa, because of the absence of an effective underground organisation.' In 1982, while based in Maputo, Mozambique, his wife, Ruth First was killed by a parcel bomb.

With the collapse of the communist system in Eastern Europe, Slovo's admiration for Stalinism required some adjustment. Stalinism, he maintained, had become 'socialism without democracy' and consequently failed. The failure occurred not because socialism itself was flawed but because 'it became separated from democracy'. Indeed, socialism remained the objective. 'If socialism is not the answer for the "wretched of the earth", then there is no answer.' As general secretary, then chairman of the South African Communist Party, as well as its leading theoretician, Slovo led the way in redefining the party's role in South Africa, with its new-found commitment to multiparty democracy.

Upon his return from exile, South Africans found not so much a demon figure as a softly-spoken, grey-haired, genial and avuncular man in his sixties who performed well on television and even had a few kind words to say about de Klerk: 'I think he is a skilled person, a talented person. He's got a greater sense of pragmatism than his predecessors, more of a sense of realism, and that explains why he did what he did. He did break with the past.'

Slovo's own sense of pragmatism, his understanding of white fears, was crucial in leading the ANC towards compromise in negotiations over the interim constitution. His proposal for a 'sunset clause' offering compulsory power-sharing succeeded in breaking the log-jam in 1992, though it lost him the respect of many radicals. He was equally pragmatic about the powerful position of the security forces, accepting the need for an amnesty even though it would probably indemnify the killers of his wife, Ruth First. 'The past cannot hang like an albatross around one's neck.'

Beyond the election, the focus of Slovo's attention is on 'economic democracy' – economic empowerment. 'A future South Africa in which all adults have the vote and can cast a ballot once every few years for a party of their choice, but in which the present economic realities cannot be changed, will be a profoundly undemocratic South Africa.' Slovo holds fast to radical solutions to the problems, but recognises the difficulties involved. 'Change will have to be gradual.'

Chapter 11

The New Agenda

The developing of democracy in South Africa is likely to be as complex as its birth. So many promises, so many demands, so many priorities, so many expectations, so many tensions confront the new government that they will stretch its abilities to the full. Not only does a new national administration, capable of undertaking major programmes of economic and social development, have to be properly established, but a whole new structure of provincial and local government as well, involving the incorporation of former homeland territories into nine new provinces and the redesign of some 800 segregated local authorities into 300 new multiracial municipal governments. The defence forces are undergoing their own transformation, with programmes of integration bringing Umkhonto we Sizwe personnel and former homeland forces into a new National Defence Force. The police service is also being overhauled to make it more amenable to local communities.

The climate of political stability which the election produced enhances the prospect of these massive changes being accomplished with a reasonable degree of order. So peaceful was the transfer of power that it brought about a swift resurgence of confidence in the future among the white community, on whose skills, expertise and capital the fortunes of South Africa still mainly depend. Whatever uncertainties the advent of majority rule involved, it seemed far more preferable to many whites than the turmoil of the last few years of white rule. How long the climate of stability lasts will be determined largely by how effectively Mandela's government delivers on its pledges on jobs, housing, education and land. This second struggle – for economic advancement – promises to be even more difficult than the struggle for political rights. The outcome depends above all, on skilful economic management.

South Africa possesses considerable assets with which to fashion its future. These include one of the world's richest stores of minerals, with 44 per cent of world diamond reserves, 82 per cent of manganese reserves and 64 per cent of platinum-group metal reserves. It is the world's largest producer of gold, mining one third of world production, with annual gold exports worth about R20 billion. Its financial, banking and legal systems are well-established and efficient. Its manufacturing base, though flabby and overprotected, is capable of considerable expansion. The overall quality of industrial management is high. The infrastructure of roads, railways, ports and airports is well developed. Telephone and electricity services are reliable. Universities and technikons turn out a ready supply of competent graduates. Levels of science and technology are above average for a newly industrialised economy. In times of stress and difficulty, the economy has proved resilient. Inflation, expected to average eight per cent in 1994, is under control. Foreign debt, as a result of substantial repayments since 1985, amounts to no more than US$15 billion, only about 15 per cent of gross domestic product (GDP). Though in world terms the economy is relatively small – about the size of Belgium's economy – in Africa it stands out as a giant, with a GDP equal to 75 per cent of sub-Saharan Africa's GDP, and with an economic hinterland which stretches as far north as Zaire.

Its past economic performance, however, has been less impressive. Each successive decade since the 1960s has seen a decline in GDP. In the 1960s, the economy grew at an average rate of more than five per cent. In the 1970s, the average rate fell to three per cent. In the 1980s, it slipped further to 2.2 per cent and, without a windfall from the gold-boom years of 1980–81, the figure would have been only about 1.5 per cent. The 1990s have seen even worse results. In the longest recession in its recorded history, South Africa's GDP fell by 0.5 per cent in 1990; by 0.4 per cent in 1991; and by 2.1 per cent in 1992, a disastrous performance caused mainly by drought disrupting agricultural production.

Taking population growth into account, South Africa's real material wealth per head of population declined from seven per cent growth in 1965 to minus 0.5 per cent in the 1980s to minus 2.7 per cent in 1990 and 1991. Measured in constant 1985 prices, this meant that real GDP per capita went from R3,331 in 1966, to R3,675 in 1970, to R3,985 in 1980, to R3,349 in 1992, to about R3,300 in 1993. The economy stabilised in 1993, with a GDP increase of 1.1 per cent, but this was largely due to a recovery in the agricultural sector. Over the four-year period from 1990 to 1993, the aggregate fall in GDP amounted to 1.8 per cent. Over a 30-year period, therefore, South Africa has made no real gain in material wealth per head of population.

The causes behind this 30-year decline are numerous. Part of it can be attributed to reduced demand and falling prices for South Africa's primary products from its main trading partners – the United States, Britain, Germany and Japan – as industrial economies restructured themselves. Part of it can be attributed to political and industrial unrest, to a collapse in real fixed investment, to sanctions and drought.

A significant feature has also been South Africa's high rate of population increase, of up to 2.7 per cent a year, with its impact on levels of poverty and unemployment. Whereas between 1960 and 1965 the economy's formal sector was able to absorb 81 per cent of newcomers entering the labour market, between 1985 and 1990 the proportion fell sharply to only 8.4 per cent. By 1993, it was no more than six per cent.

The fall in employment growth since the 1960s has been proportionately even greater than the fall in GDP growth, mainly as a result of decisions by the industrial sector, faced with declining labour productivity and rising labour costs, to substitute labour for capital-intensive methods of production.

The combined impact of capital intensification, difficult trading conditions and economic recession on levels of employment has been severe. Between 1988 and 1993, the gold and coal industries cut 210,000 jobs – more than one third of the workforce – depriving between four and six million people dependent on those retrenched of some form of income. Overall, formal employment between 1989 and 1993 fell by about 364,000, about 4.5 per cent of the total. Only the number of government employees increased. At the end of 1993, formal sector employment stood at only 7.72 million jobs, about half the economically active population. No net additional employment in the formal non-agricultural sectors of the economy has been gained over the past ten years.

Part of the balance has been taken up by the informal sector – hawkers, small traders, backyard businesses, domestics. Indeed, with formal sector employment contracting, the informal sector has been the main source of employment generation. For the majority of new entrants to the labour market each year, it is likely to remain their only option. About 3.5 million find work there; another one million survive through subsistence agriculture; some two million others have no direct way of making a living. Crime for many is the only means of survival.

The clamour for jobs, consequently, was at the top of the list of demands made to politicians during the election campaign; and the promise of jobs became their most consistent response. Yet the stark statistics defy any easy resolution. Of the 450,000 entrants to the labour market in 1994, only 27,000 are expected to find jobs in the formal sector. The problem is made worse by the number of unskilled people seeking employment. Two thirds of the economically active population are under-educated, without basic levels of literacy and numeracy. The increasing rate of unskilled unemployment, reaching an estimated 57 per cent by the year 2000, appears to represent an insuperable problem.

Merely to absorb the annual number of new entrants into the labour market would require an annual economic growth rate of six per cent. To make any inroads into the rate of unemployment would require a growth rate of between eight and ten per cent. Yet even the most optimistic assumptions about the average real GDP growth rate between 1994 and 1999 go no further than four per cent a year. Given the poor start that South Africa made in the early 1990s, the average annual increase in GDP for this decade as a whole is likely to be no more than 2.2 per cent. Taking population growth into account, this would mean that per capita living standards would be no higher at the end of the century than they were 35 years earlier.

Whatever efforts are made by the government, the legacy of years of economic decline, falling formal sector employment and high population growth, will be difficult to reverse. Poverty has reached chronic proportions. Almost half of the households in South Africa live below the poverty line. One quarter of all households live on an income of less than half of the poverty line income. As the Development Bank of Southern Africa has noted, some 18 million Africans are 'struggling to survive'; some eight million are 'completely destitute'. The widest spread of poverty occurs in the former homelands of Transkei, Bophuthatswana, Venda and Ciskei. More than 40 per cent of blacks live in rural areas, yet agriculture accounts for only five per cent of GDP. It has been calculated that for households currently living in poverty to reach a level above the poverty line would take 24 years with an average rate of economic growth of five per cent a year, or 40 years with an average rate of three per cent a year.

Looked at in terms of a social backlog, the figures are

equally daunting. Out of a population of 40 million, 22 million lack adequate sanitation, including 7.5 million in urban areas; 12 million lack clean water supply; 7.8 million live in shacks; more than one million are homeless; 23 million have no access to electricity; and some two million children are without schools.

The grip of poverty is no longer confined to blacks but extends to the white community. In 1975 there were no whites among the poorest fifth of households. Now five per cent fall into that category. As a study by the Human Sciences Research Council (HSRC) and the University of Natal, published in 1994, shows, it was the poorest ten per cent of whites who suffered the steepest decline in incomes, in relative terms, between 1975 and 1991; by 1991 their median income was 28 per cent of what it had been in 1975, falling from R15,918 to R4,533. The poorest 40 per cent of the white population have seen their incomes drop by a percentage similar to that of the poorest 40 per cent of blacks.

In the 1990s, a new income gap is emerging. The old gap between white and black, which has been the root cause of so much political strife, still remains. The average income of a white household is twelve times greater than the average of a black household, a figure similar to that in the 1960s when a huge widening of the gap in income between white and black developed. Whites, comprising 13 per cent of the population, earn 61 per cent of total income. During the recession, the richest category of whites managed to hold their own, unlike many others.

In recent years, however, a similar gap has been developing within the black population. In 1975, less than ten per cent of the richest 20 per cent of South African households were black. By 1991, according to the HSRC report, this figure had risen to 26 per cent. The black share of total income is still comparatively small. In 1991, blacks, comprising 75 per cent of the population, earned 28 per cent of total income, a rise from 20 per cent in 1970. But their rising share of total income is attributable mainly to the large increases in incomes of the richest black households. The richest 20 per cent of black households increased their real average incomes between 1975 and 1991 by almost 40 per cent, making them the most upwardly mobile group; while over the same period the poorest 40 per cent of blacks slid ever deeper into poverty, with median incomes falling by over 42 per cent. Inequality in South Africa, according to the HSRC report, is no longer mainly attributable to the gap between white and black, but to the gap within population groups. Class divisions are thus as likely to be the cause of conflict in the future as racial divisions. As the HSRC report noted: 'The possibility now exists that the emerging income gap among blacks may threaten the viability of a democratically elected government, in the same way that the reaction to the white-black gap served to undermine apartheid.'

The advent of a new government determined to erase the legacy of inequality between black and white is bound to provide further impetus to the development of a wealthy black élite, however much Mandela's administration tries to focus attention on the poorer sections of society. In the civil service and parastatal companies, the aim is to ensure blacks gain positions of status and responsibility from which they have been barred for so long. The private sector is anxious to follow suit and similarly redress the record. Despite lengthy debates about affirmative action, blacks still hold no more than ten per cent of all managerial posts, and only 50 out of more than 2,500 directorships counted in a survey of big business boardrooms. The prospects for the black middle class are thus highly promising. The unions, for their part, intend to flex their muscles in quest of better wages and conditions and workplace 'empowerment'. But, like the black middle class, they represent a privileged minority.

To meet the demands of the broader population, the

government plans a huge public works programme, concentrating on housing, electrification, sewerage and water supply, providing a massive boost to employment levels. The advantages of house-building programmes, in particular, are that not only do they tackle a desperate social need and raise employment, but they offer the fastest means available of meeting pent-up expectations aroused by the election. The housing backlog, taking its lowest estimate, is 1.4 million homes. In 1993, the number of new housing units built by the state was fewer than 30,000. In order to eliminate the present housing shortage and cater for new market entrants, an average of 338,000 units needs to be built each year over the next ten years. Given the current capacity problems of the building industry, a realistic target for 1995 would be 100,000 units, rising to about 300,000 units three years later. But an even more formidable constraint occurs over finance. The annual construction of 338,000 units would cost R9 billion a year. The most the government could probably afford to provide is about R4 billion, or about four per cent of the national budget, a sizeable figure given all the other demands on the government's resources. The rest would have to come from the private sector, which is wary of the risks involved in township development. Even with such public job-creation projects, the impact on existing unemployment levels, though substantial, will not be dramatic. Building 100,000 house units would provide about 350,000 jobs for a limited period, equal to about three quarters of the number of new entrants coming on to the labour market each year.

As the housing example illustrates, the ability of the ANC-led government to fulfil its ambitions and to deliver on its election promises, rests in large part on the response of the private sector, in particular its willingness to commit large sums for investment in social programmes. A World Bank study in 1993 calculated that, providing there was a strong resurgence of private sector investment, then South Africa should be able to achieve a sustainable growth path of above five per cent a year, with low inflation, a stable fiscal account and low and stable debt-to-GDP ratios. The fiscal deficit, it estimated, would remain at about ten per cent of GDP for a few years, then fall as growth continued into the early part of the next century, turning into a small surplus. External borrowing would not exceed about two per cent of GDP in any year before 2001, when it would climb to between four and five per cent. The government would be able to invest R70 billion (at 1985 prices) between 1994 and 2005, around 3.3 per cent of GDP annually, in areas such as infrastructure, education and health care.

Without private sector investment, all other steps taken by a new government would count for little. The economy would experience higher growth for a few years, peaking at around two per cent GDP growth, but then start to drop precipitously. Formal sector unemployment, after a brief dip, would head off to new heights by the end of the 1990s. The government would be forced to curtail public expenditure abruptly, creating a negative demand shock leading to a new recession. The World Bank study calculated that in the absence of restored business confidence, and without private investment to complement other essential initiatives, especially to upgrade black skills, the government would forgo R30 billion over the next ten years to invest in improving black living standards and prospects.

Yet the ANC came to office bearing suspicion and mistrust of the white business sector. Some ANC politicians see it as the next redoubt to be captured. Protected by apartheid laws, South Africa's whites control about 90 per cent of formal business, as well as almost 90 per cent of land. Years of political and economic isolation have helped bring about a huge concentration of economic power. Six conglomerates control almost 90 per cent of publicly listed companies, producing about half of South Africa's GDP. One empire alone, the Anglo American and de Beers group, belonging to the Oppenheimer family, controls about one third of stock-market capitalisation.

The contrast with the position of the black business community is stark. Barely two per cent of all private sector assets are black owned. Most black business operates in the informal sector where it is constrained by lack of access to capital, business skills and infrastructure. Only two black firms rank among industry leaders: National Sorghum Breweries, and African Life, the country's seventh largest insurer, acquired by a consortium of black investors in February 1994. Only one of about 750 companies listed on the Johannesburg Stock Exchange is owned by blacks.

Aware of the need to encourage black ownership, the white business community is attempting to facilitate the entry of black business into the higher realms of the economy, in much the same way that 'English' capital helped the Afrikaner business community to gain a foothold in the mining industry in the 1960s. The crucial transaction then was the sale of a company called General Mining which by the 1990s had become South Africa's second largest mining house. One candidate being considered as a vehicle for 'unbundling', with 'black empowerment' in mind, is an Anglo American-linked conglomerate, Johannesburg Consolidated Investment. The difficulty with performing the same task with the black business community in the 1990s is that, whereas the Afrikaner business community has developed a long tradition of savings and capital formation and possessed at least some wealth, blacks have had little opportunity to accrue wealth, still less to save it. The concern is that the process might merely enable the same small group of successful black businessmen, who have gained a foothold in the world of big business, to further enrich themselves. In one deal after another, the same names are already recurring.

While expressing support for many of the ANC's objectives, the business community has remained sceptical about the methods it might use to attain them. Above all, there has been concern about the persistent lack of clarity surrounding the ANC's intentions, as it has twisted and turned, trying to satisfy different audiences. Assurances given one day have been contradicted the next. A main fear has been that the ANC-led government would face intense pressure to deliver its promises more rapidly and in greater quantities than sensible economics permit, raising the spectre of hyperinflation, a debt trap and balance of payments crises. The degree of uncertainty about ANC policies has had a double impact: not only have South African businessmen delayed decisions on investment, but foreign investors have followed suit. Until the domestic business community gains sufficient confidence to invest in the future, direct foreign investment is likely to steer clear.

Even given the goodwill of the business community, the impediments to the government's reconstruction programme are formidable. The levels of both gross domestic fixed investment and gross domestic savings are chronically low, far too low for any hopes of high and sustained long-term economic growth. Gross domestic fixed investment has been falling for five years. It reached an all-time low of 14.5 per cent of GDP in 1993. In real terms, capital stock has risen less than seven per cent since 1985. The International Monetary Fund estimates that for South Africa to rebuild its level of fixed investment would leave hardly any scope for increases in average real wages at least until the year 2000. For aggregate savings to grow as a percentage of GDP would require a reduction in aggregate consumption as a percentage of GDP, in particular government consumption. The most critical component of government consumption spending is the public wage and salary bill. One in four people employed in the formal sector is employed by the government. The wage bill of government has constituted between 61 and 66 per cent of current expenditure since 1984. Indeed, it was the public sector which acted as 'market leaders' in real wage packets between 1971 and 1990. Just when the public sector is being fully opened to black participation, what good economic management requires is a cutback in its payroll.

South Africa has also been plagued by persistent outflows of capital, with damaging effects on economic activity. Between 1985 and 1993 the cumulative net outflow was R49 billion. A large proportion of this – R16 billion – occurred in 1993 as foreign confidence in South Africa's future waned. A major factor again was concern about the ANC's economic policies, in particular fears over expropriation, increased restrictions, higher taxation and reduced value as a result of excessive currency depreciation. Although South Africa managed a current account surplus of R7 billion in 1993, the capital outflow left a R9 billion gap to be met through a run-down of reserves and increased foreign borrowing. Currency reserves of about R10 billion at the end of 1993 were equal to about six weeks' imports, half the internationally accepted norm of three months. This not only prevented interest rate cuts but threatened the whole process of economic recovery. Capital outflows continued into 1994 as political uncertainty and internal conflict led foreign lenders and investors to withdraw further funds. By April the reserves had fallen to R7.3 billion. The main hope of Reserve Bank officials is that in the second half of 1994 there will be a reversal in capital outflows, or at least a decline, with the prospect that net capital flows might be neutral by 1995.

The outflow of capital would have been even greater but for exchange controls and South Africa's use of a dual currency system, involving a commercial rand for normal commercial activity, and a financial rand for non-resident investors, designed to protect the country's reserves. Reserve Bank officials estimate that the pool of non-resident financial rand balances, awaiting an exit but currently blocked by exchange controls, amounts to R4 billion. Because the financial rand tends to penalise repatriation of capital, it acts as a deterrent to foreign investment. The government's aim is to abolish it as soon as circumstances allow. But with foreign reserves under threat and substantial debt repayments due, there is no prospect of abolition in sight. The prospect of other exchange controls being lifted is even more remote. Foreign investors, meanwhile, remain wary.

The government's scope for financing reconstruction through higher taxation is strictly limited, as the ANC recognises. The government already absorbs one third of the country's earnings, with taxation levels close to the limit of what can be imposed without causing a skills flight and other economic damage. Individuals already shoulder 44 per cent of the tax burden. According to the International Monetary Fund, middle-income South Africans are among the most highly taxed in the world. Of the rest, company taxes provide 14 per cent; value-added tax, 22 per cent; customs and import duties, nine per cent and fuel levies, eight per cent. In the budget projections for fiscal year 1994–95 (Mandela's first budget), taxation from these sources is intended to raise in all R99 billion, leaving a deficit of R26 billion or 6.4 per cent of GDP, close to the target agreed with the International Monetary Fund. The gross financing requirement for 1994–95 is R33 billion. The intention is to raise R1.5 billion of this offshore and the remaining R31.5 billion through the issue of government stock. But the continued high levels of government borrowing to finance the deficit is in itself placing a heavy burden on the exchequer. The interest on public debt in 1994–95 is expected to reach more than R23 billion.

As for shifting expenditure into areas favoured by the ANC, considerable movement has already occurred and the scope for further increases is limited. Between 1988–89 and 1993–94, spending on social services rose from 39 per cent of total expenditure to 44 per cent, with the education budget growing from 18.2 per cent to 21.1 per cent, and health from 9.3 per cent to 10.6 per cent. On housing it fell from 1.4 per cent to 1.2 per cent of the total. Most of the higher expenditure on social services was achieved at the expense of defence, police and prison services whose share of the total dropped from 20.7 per cent to 17.6 per cent. In order to increase capital spending on schools, houses and clinics by reducing current expenditure, the government would need to impose wage restraints.

Aggravating all the government's difficulties is the constant pressure of population growth. By the year 2018 the population is expected to double from its present size to 80 million, about the maximum number of people South Africa's natural resources can support. The rate of urbanisation is likely to be even higher. Already, the rate of black population increase in metropolitan areas, at about 4.5 per cent, far exceeds the natural rate of increase, which was as high as 2.6 per cent throughout the 1980s. In Cape Town, the black population growth rate of 13 per cent a year over the past decade has made it one of the fastest growing cities in Africa. Overall, the urban population is expected to grow from its present 57 per cent of the total population to 70 per cent by 2010, with about 50 per cent of the black population living in four main metropolitan areas. The strain on urban resources is already immense.

Despite all the obstacles, the ANC's objectives are still attainable. What is required is a magic combination of political stability; sound economic management; an investor-friendly climate; solid business confidence; wage restraint; rising productivity and competitiveness; successful export drives; and a reduction in population growth.

Even so, South Africa's new era has begun in far more auspicious circumstances than once seemed possible. Transforming South Africa into a democracy has been an achievement of such magnitude that it makes the problems of the future appear less daunting. On 10 May 1994 South Africans all over the country celebrated that achievement with a sense of national pride they had never felt before and watched with awe the moment of history when Nelson Mandela, before an audience of world leaders in front of Union Buildings in Pretoria, took the oath of office and promised South Africans a new covenant.

'We enter into a covenant that we shall build a society in which all South Africans, both black and white, will be able to walk tall, without any fear in their hearts, assured of their inalienable right to human dignity – a rainbow nation at peace with itself and the world.'

Appendix:

Members of the Government of National Unity (May 1994)

President
Nelson Mandela, ANC, 75. Lawyer, Robben Islander. Co-founder of ANC Youth League, 1944; chief organiser of Defiance Campaign; treason trialist; first commander of Umkhonto we Sizwe; arrested, 1962; sentenced to life imprisonment, 1964; released, 1990; joint Nobel Peace Prize winner with de Klerk, 1993.

First Deputy President
Thabo Mbeki, ANC, 52. Exiled leader. Student activist; went into exile, 1962; studied economics at the University of Sussex, England; military training in the Soviet Union, 1970; head of ANC's international affairs department; lapsed SACP member; returned from exile, 1990

Second Deputy President
F. W. de Klerk, NP, 58. Lawyer, former State President. Member of parliament, 1972; cabinet minister, 1978; leader of the National Party, 1989; State President, 1989; joint Nobel Peace Prize winner with Mandela, 1993.

Minister of Justice
Dullah Omar, ANC, 59. Civil rights lawyer. Studied at University of Cape Town; member of Mandela's legal

team during his prison days; former United Democratic Front (UDF) official; detained, 1985; former director of Community Law Centre at the University of Western Cape.

Minister of Defence
Joe Modise, ANC, 65. Exiled leader. Treason trialist. Former commander of Umkhonto we Sizwe, 1965–93; trained in Czechoslovakia and Soviet Union; key figure in integration of Umkhonto we Sizwe (MK) forces into new National Defence Force.

Minister of Safety and Security (Police)
Sydney Mufamadi, ANC/SACP, 35. Trade unionist. Student activist; former UDF official; assistant general secretary of Cosatu, 1985; SACP delegate at Codesa.

Minister of Education
Sibusiso Bhengu, ANC, 54. Teacher. Studied at University of Zululand, professor, dean; first secretary-general of Inkatha, 1975; broke with Buthelezi, 1978; spent twelve years at Geneva headquarters of World Lutheran Federation; first black rector of the University of Fort Hare, 1991.

Minister of Trade and Industry
Trevor Manuel, ANC, 38. Civil engineering technician, community activist in Western Cape. Former UDF official; several periods of imprisonment, 1985–89; head of ANC's department of economic planning.

Minister of Foreign Affairs
Alfred Nzo, ANC, 68. Exiled leader. Joined ANC Youth League at Fort Hare University, 1946; former health inspector; Defiance Campaign activist; Freedom Charter participant; went into exile, 1964; posted to India, Egypt, Zambia and Tanzania; ANC general secretary, 1969–91.

Minister of Labour
Tito Mboweni, ANC, 35. Economist, former exile. Studied at the University of Lesotho and the University of East Anglia; deputy head of the ANC's Department of Economic Planning.

Minister of Posts, Telecommunications and Broadcasting
Pallo Jordan, ANC, 51. Former exile. Studied at University of Wisconsin and London School of Economics; worked for ANC Department of Information and Publicity (DIP) in London, Angola, Zambia, 1975–1989; head, DIP, from 1989. Independent socialist intellectual.

Minister of Health
Nkosazana Zuma, ANC, 45. Paediatrician. Studied zoology and botany, University of Zululand; medicine at the University of Natal, Bristol University, and School of Tropical Medicine in Liverpool; specialist in tropical child health.

Minister of Transport
Mac Maharaj, ANC, 59. Robben Islander. Sentenced to twelve years' imprisonment on charges of sabotage, 1964; went into exile, 1976; active underground in South Africa, 1987–90; lapsed SACP member; key figure in constitutional negotiations.

Minister of Provincial Affairs and Constitutional Development
Roelf Meyer, NP, 46. Lawyer. Member of parliament, 1979; appointed minister, 1992; government's chief negotiator in constitutional negotiations, established effective working relatiship with ANC's chief negotiator, Cyril Ramaphosa.

Minister of Land Affairs
Derek Hanekom, ANC, 40. Agricultural economist; farmer. Studied at University of Pretoria; imprisoned for two

years for ANC involvement, 1983; head of ANC's land commission.

Minister of Public Enterprises
Stella Sigcau, ANC, 56. Teacher. Member of parliament, Transkei, 1968; first State President, Transkei, 1987; overthrown after 86 days in office by military coup led by General Bantubonke Holomisa.

Minister of Public Service and Administration
Zola Skweyiya, ANC, 48. Lawyer, former exile. Studied at Fort Hare University and Leipzig University; head of ANC's Department of Legal and Constitutional Affairs and its Civil Service Unit.

Minister of Housing
Joe Slovo, ANC/SACP, 68. Lawyer, exiled leader. Communist activist since 1940s; founding member of Congress of Democrats, 1953; contributor to Freedom Charter, 1955; treason trialist; went into exile, 1964; chief of staff of Umkhonto we Sizwe; returned 1990; SACP chairman.

Minister of Public Works
Jeff Radebe, ANC/SACP, 41. Lawyer, former exile, Robben Islander. Studied at University of Zululand; left South Africa, 1977; studied at Leipzig University; based in Tanzania, Zambia and Lesotho; arrested on mission in South Africa, 1986, sentenced to six years' imprisonment; released, 1990.

Minister of Correctional Services
Sipho Mzimela, IFP, 59. Teacher, Episcopalian priest. Former ANC activist; went into exile, 1961, trained in Tanzania and Czechoslovakia; ANC's deputy representative at United Nations, 1977–80; quit in protest over SACP alliance, 1985; joined Inkatha, 1990; former Inkatha US representative.

Minister of Finance
Derek Keys, NP, 63. Chartered accountant. Executive chairman, Gencor, South Africa's second largest mining house, 1986–91; appointed Minister of Trade, Industry and Economic Co-ordination, 1992; Minister of Finance, 1992; highly respected financial manager.

Minister of Agriculture
Kraai van Niekerk, NP, 55. Farmer, agricultural research scientist. Member of parliament, 1981; Deputy Minister of Agriculture, 1986; Minister of Agriculture, 1991.

Minister for Sports and Recreation
Steve Tshwete, ANC, 56. Robben Islander. Student activist; charged with sabotage, sentenced to 15 years' imprisonment, 1964; UDF official; went into exile, 1985; MK political commissar; returned 1990; played a major role in sports integration and in assisting South Africa's return to international sport.

Minister of Home Affairs
Mangosuthu Buthelezi, IFP, 65. Leader of Inkatha Freedom Party. Chief executive officer, KwaZulu Territorial Authority, 1970; founded Inkatha cultural movement, 1975; Chief Minister of KwaZulu, 1976–94.

Minister of Water Affairs and Forestry
Kader Asmal, ANC, 59. Teacher, lawyer, former exile. Anti-apartheid activist in Britain and Ireland, 1960–90; former professor of human rights at the University of Western Cape.

Minister of Environmental Affairs and Tourism
Dawie de Villiers, NP, 53. Former Dutch Reformed Church dominie, teacher. Member of parliament, 1972–79; ambassador to London, 1979–80; cabinet minister, 1980–94.

Minister of Mineral and Energy Affairs
'Pik' Botha, NP, 62. Lawyer, diplomat. Served in South African Department of Foreign Affairs, 1953–70; member of parliament, 1970–74; UN representative, 1975–77; Minister of Foreign Affairs, 1977–94.

Minister of Welfare and Population Development
Abe Williams, NP, 54. Teacher. Sportsman and sports administrator; one of the first Coloured politicians to join NP; member of tricameral parliament, 1984; deputy minister, 1989; joined de Klerk's cabinet as Sports Minister, 1993.

Minister of Arts, Culture, Science and Technology
Ben Ngubane, IFP, 52. Medical doctor. Former Minister of Health in KwaZulu government; KwaZulu government's chief negotiator in constitutional negotiations.

Minister without Portfolio
Jay Naidoo, ANC, 39. Trade unionist. Community worker in predominantly Indian areas in late 1970s; founding general secretary of labour federation, Congress of South African Trade Unions, 1985; co-ordinator of ANC's Reconstruction and Development Programme, for which he is now responsible.

Provincial Premiers

PWV (Pretoria-Witwatersrand-Vereeniging)
Tokyo Sexwale, ANC, 41. Robben Islander, former exile. Born in Orlando, Soweto; joined ANC underground at the age of 18; went into exile in 1975; military training in Soviet Union; arrested in cross-border MK mission in 1977; served twelve years on Robben Island, where he met his lawyer wife, Judy van Vuuren; released in 1990; highly respected by business leaders.

Northern Transvaal
Ngoako Ramatlhodi, ANC, 38. Lawyer, former exile. Student activist; went into exile in 1980; MK regional commissar in Lesotho; speech-writer for Oliver Tambo; obtained law degree at University of Zimbabwe; returned to South Africa in 1990; lecturer in public international law at the University of the North.

Eastern Transvaal
Mathews Phosa, ANC, 42. Lawyer, former exile. Practised in Nelspruit after graduating from the University of the North; went into exile in 1985; received political, military and intelligence training in East Germany; stationed in Mozambique as commander of MK border units; returned to South Africa in 1990.

North West
Popo Molefe, ANC, 42. Graduate of 1976 Soweto uprising; detained, 1976; former UDF national secretary; detained, 1985; charged with treason at the Delmas treason trial; sentenced to ten years imprisonment in 1988; released on appeal in 1989.

Northern Cape
Manne Dipico, ANC, 35. Trade unionist. Studied at Fort Hare University; regional organiser of the National Union of Mineworkers; UDF activist; sentenced to five years' imprisonment in 1987 for ANC underground activity; released in 1990.

Western Cape
Hernus Kriel, NP, 52. Lawyer. Studied at University of Stellenbosch; entered parliament in 1984; appointed cabinet minister in 1989. Former Minister of Law and Order.

Eastern Cape
Raymond Mhlaba, 74, ANC/SACP. Robben Islander. Defiance Campaign leader; treason trialist; member of MK

high command; arrested at Lilliesleaf farm in 1963; imprisoned along with Mandela on Robben Island; released in 1989, national deputy chairman of SACP.

Orange Free State
Patrick Lekota, ANC, 46. Robben Islander. Student activist; sentenced to six years' imprisonment on Robben Island; released in 1982; UDF activist; charged with treason at Delmas treason trial; sentenced to twelve years' imprisonment in 1988; released on appeal in 1989; nicknamed 'Terror' as a result of his skills at football.

KwaZulu/Natal
Frank Mdlalose, IFP, 62. Medical doctor. Active in ANC Youth League in 1950s; joined Inkatha at its launch in 1975; spent 16 years as minister in KwaZulu government; national chairman of Inkatha.

Acknowledgements

This account of South Africa's turbulent transition to democracy, written during the 1994 election campaign, has made extensive use of South Africa's press and publications of the time. This has included: *The Star, Business Day, The Citizen, Sowetan, Sunday Times, Weekly Mail & Guardian, Financial Mail, Finance Week, Indicator Project South Africa, Leadership,* and *Work in Progress*. The literature on modern South Africa is too vast to record here but a number of recent books deserve mention: William de Klerk's biography of his brother, *F. W. de Klerk: The Man in his Time*, Jonathan Ball, Johannesburg, 1991; Steven Friedman's account of the Codesa negotiations, *The Long Journey: South Africa's Quest for a Negotiated Settlement*, Ravan Press, Johannesburg, 1993; Shelagh Gastrow's *Who's Who in South African Politics*, Johannesburg, 1992; Emma Gilbey's *The Lady: The Life and Times of Winnie Mandela*, Cape, London 1993; Shaun Johnson's collection of his newspaper columns, *Strange Days Indeed*, Bantam, Johannesburg, 1993; and the 1993-94 *Race Relations Survey* by the South African Institute of Race Relations, Johannesburg, 1994. My thanks are due to the librarian and staff at the South African Institute of International Affairs, Jan Smuts House, University of the Witwatersrand, for their unfailing assistance.

MM
Johannesburg, May 1994

SPECIALIST ADVISORY GROUP ON AFRICA

The Specialist Advisory Group on Africa is a business, political and economic intelligence network. It provides strategic information and political analysis to help businesses make decisions in a climate of high opportunity and high risk. It is controlled by partners in London and Johannesburg.

How SAGA can help businesses interested in investing in South Africa

- Political advice
  SAGA has extensive political connections and can provide quality political analysis of the risks to potential and existing investors

- Client service
  SAGA provides a tailored client service. This includes political and economic confidential briefs on a one-off or ongoing basis

- Consultants
  SAGA has a comprehensive list of consultants and advisers working in all sectors.

To find out more about the Specialist Advisory Group on Africa please contact:
London
26 Glenmore Road, London NW3 4DB Tel: 071 722 3862 Fax: 071 722 5018

Johannesburg
7th Floor, Hallmark Towers, 54 Siemert Road, Doornfontein 2094 Fax: 011 402 0060

A Selected List of Non-Fiction Titles Available from Mandarin

While every effort is made to keep prices low, it is sometimes necessary to increase prices at short notice. Mandarin Paperbacks reserves the right to show new retail prices on covers which may differ from those previously advertised in the text or elsewhere.

The prices shown below were correct at the time of going to press.

☐	7493 0692 0	**A History of God**	Karen Armstrong	£6.99
☐	7493 1028 6	**In the Psychiatrist's Chair**	Anthony Clare	£5.99
☐	7493 0186 4	**The Sign and the Seal**	Graham Hancock	£5.99
☐	7493 0497 9	**All Right OK You Win**	David Spanier	£5.99
☐	7493 0887 7	**The British Constitution Now**	Ferdinand Mount	£6.99
☐	7493 0618 1	**Justice Delayed**	David Cesarani	£5.99
☐	7493 1031 6	**Catholics and Sex**	Saunders/Stanford	£4.99
☐	7493 1491 5	**Erotic Life of the Married Woman**	Dalma Heyn	£4.99
☐	7493 1412 5	**Sexual Arrangements**	Reibstein/Richards	£4.99
☐	7493 1102 9	**Italian Neighbours**	Tim Parks	£5.99
☐	7493 1254 8	**A Spell in Wild France**	Bill/Laurel Cooper	£5.99
☐	7493 1328 5	**Among the Thugs**	Bill Buford	£4.99
☐	7493 0961 X	**Stick it up Your Punter**	Chippendale & Horrib	£4.99
☐	7493 0938 5	**The Courage to Heal**	Ellen Bass and Laura Davis	£7.99
☐	7493 0637 8	**The Hollywood Story**	Joel Finler	£9.99
☐	7493 1172 X	**You'll Never Eat Lunch in This Town Again**	Julia Phillips	£5.99

All these books are available at your bookshop or newsagent, or can be ordered direct from the address below. Just tick the titles you want and fill in the form below.

Cash Sales Department, PO Box 5, Rushden, Northants NN10 6YX.
Fax: 0933 410321 : Phone 0933 410511.

Please send cheque, payable to 'Reed Book Services Ltd.', or postal order for purchase price quoted and allow the following for postage and packing:

£1.00 for the first book, 50p for the second; **FREE POSTAGE AND PACKING FOR THREE BOOKS OR MORE PER ORDER.**

NAME (Block letters) ....

ADDRESS ....

....

☐ I enclose my remittance for ....

☐ I wish to pay by Access/Visa Card Number

Expiry Date

Signature ....

Please quote our reference: MAND